Praise for *Saving Your Assets When You Can't Save Your Marriage*

"If you have assets and want to keep them, you need this book. *Saving Your Assets* is a must read book to help deal with the stress and emotion of a divorce."

Elise Smith Chatham,
Family and Life Consultant

"Authors Wood and Shaw have done an excellent job of writing a guidebook on divorce that covers all the critical issues. This book should be required reading for anyone contemplating a divorce."

Stewart Welch, III
Wealth Manager

"It's difficult to keep emotions from affecting financial decisions you must make during a divorce. This book will help!"

Mary Wier
Certified Divorce Planner

"*Saving Your Assets* contains valuable principles to help you protect your financial future."

Dawn Peeples
Financial Representative

"*Saving Your Assets* is the most practical and clearly written book on the subject of money and divorce in Alabama. To keep the assets you have, read this book."

Jeff Hammock
Private Investigator
Comprehensive Investigative Group

Successful Financial Divorce in Alabama

Saving Your Assets
When You Can't
Save Your Marriage

John M. Wood
Paul B. Shaw, Jr.
Attorneys at Law

Published by PSG Books
Dallas, Texas

Saving Your Assets
When You Can't Save Your Marriage

John M. Wood and Paul B. Shaw, Jr.

Edited by Larry Upshaw
PSG Books
9830 Kingsley Road, #405   Dallas, Texas 75238
214/340-6223   214/343-9063 fax
upshaw@onramp.net

Books published under the imprint of PSG Books are distributed to the U.S. book trade by Hervey's Booklink, 10265 Miller Road, Dallas, Texas 75238, phone 214/221-2711, fax 214/221-2715. Resellers outside the book trade who wish reprints or quantity discounts can contact PSG Books at 800/465-1508.

Authors John M. Wood and Paul B. Shaw, Jr. are available to speak to groups on the financial aspects of divorce. They can be reached at Wood & Shaw, L.L.C., 2924 Crescent Avenue, Birmingham, Alabama 35209, phone 205/871-9550, fax 205/871-9549, email: info@woodandshaw.com, website: www.woodandshaw.com.

ISBN 0-9659273-3-4

Manufactured in the United States of America

9 8 7 6 5 4 3 2 1

NOTICE

State laws, legal precedents, tax codes and regulations vary greatly from one jurisdiction to another and change over time. Because of this, the reader should not use this book for specific legal advice. Every divorce case and post-divorce action is unique, requiring the advice of those versed in the laws of the jurisdiction where the action is taken. It must be understood, therefore, that this book will provide readers with a general overview of financial matters related to the divorce process and post-divorce issues, so they may take legal action or otherwise address these issues better informed. This book is not intended to provide legal advice. You should consult an attorney for specific information related to your personal situation.

People described in this book are not meant to represent any person living or deceased. No true names or actual fact patterns have been used by the authors except where full names are given.

Any similarities between actual people or situations and the characters described in this book are purely coincidental.

TABLE OF CONTENTS

PART ONE
Divorce Planning:
Where, When and How to Begin

Nine Basic Truths of an Alabama Divorce

No Short-Term Fix … The Decision is Made …
Prenuptial Agreements … Enforcing Your Prenup …
Socking Away Information … Hiding Money, Tracing
Assets … Spying, Sneaking and Snooping Can Uncover
the Truth … Split Decisions

How Wide the War? … Keeping Your Spouse as a Friend
… When Your Spouse Becomes the Enemy … Planning
Your Divorce Strategy … Sometimes Fault Breaks a Tie
… Alternative Dispute Resolution … Growing
Importance of Mediation … Explaining the Process …
Beware of Mediation Abusers

PART TWO

Settlement:
Dividing Assets, Absorbing Debt

Alternatives to Bankruptcy ... Advice from a Victim of
Uncontrollable Debt

PART THREE

Details of the Divorce: Providing for the Future

ABOUT THE AUTHORS

John M. Wood and Paul B. Shaw, Jr. are partners in the Birmingham, Alabama law firm of Wood & Shaw, L.L.C. Their firm's practice is heavily concentrated in family law, including child custody and divorce litigation. Their objective in writing *Saving Your Assets When You Can't Save Your Marriage* is to emphasize that divorce is often the single most important financial transaction an individual will experience. The outcome can affect not only the husband and wife, but the children and extended family members as well. For John and Paul, the goal is to provide the reader with a resource to begin the analysis of their own situation.

John is the author of *The Successful Divorce*, published in 1997. This book is in its third printing and is being revised for a second edition. John is married and the father of two girls. He is an active member of Liberty Park Baptist Church and supports many charities. John graduated from Georgetown University Law School. He is a member of the American Bar Association and is the former chairman of the Alabama State Bar Family Law Section. He currently serves as a member of the Family Law Section Executive Committee and is a member of the Birmingham Bar Association.

Paul B. Shaw, Jr. has combined his concentration in family law with his experience in civil and business litigation. In more than 14 years of practice, Paul has represented several Fortune 500 Companies, some of them based in Birmingham. His business representation and litigation experience helps him deal with large asset or business-based divorce cases and forms much of the basis for the financial perspective displayed in this book. Paul is married and the father of two girls. He is a member of Asbury United Methodist Church and has been recognized by the National Multiple Sclerosis Society for his accomplishments in charitable and community service. Paul is a graduate of the University of Alabama Law School and received a degree in economics from Auburn University. He is a member of the Alabama Bar Association, the Mississippi Bar Association and the Birmingham Bar Association. He has served as Co-chairman of the Alabama Family Law Section State Bar Committee and as a member of that section's Executive Committee.

John and Paul frequently speak on family law issues at seminars and workshops. They've also appeared numerous times on state and local media. Each has been honored by the *Birmingham Business Journal* as one of the city's *Top 40 Under 40,* recognizing young leaders in the business and civic arena.

— The Publisher

ACKNOWLEDGMENTS

A book like this is never the product of just one or two people. We want to thank our clients for putting their trust in us by allowing us to work on their cases and affect their lives. Without these experiences, we would not be able to knowledgeably approach the subject of the financial side of divorce.

Thanks also to the many area attorneys, judges and other professionals who contributed their expertise to the book or critiqued our work prior to publication. This is especially true of financial planner Stewart Welch, III, and certified divorce planner Mary Wier.

Special thanks to our editor, Larry Upshaw, for his attention to detail. If it's possible, he showed more care with this book than he did with the first one, *The Successful Divorce*.

And a most profound thank you to our families, friends and staff members who put up with our minor obsession to complete this book and do it right. Support on every front is essential when you run a law firm by day and create nonfiction by night.

— The Authors

FOREWORD
By Stewart H. Welch, III

Divorce happens to approximately half the marriages in America, resulting in a financial and emotional "ripple effect" that can be felt for years, even generations.

People often describe the experience as worse than living through the death of someone you love. It is a situation that is typically charged with emotion, with significant financial issues at stake. Emotion often helps to drive the financial issues as spouses attempt to grab assets and inflict pain on their soon-to-be ex-husbands or wives. All too often, the result is fewer assets to be divided among the divorcing spouses.

If you are contemplating a divorce, carefully think through the ramifications to you, your family and your finances. If children are involved, this decision becomes that much more critical. If you have made a decision to get a divorce, take appropriate steps to make sure you end up with the best agreement possible. To obtain this result, you need to develop a "success" mindset where you think of your personal finances as a business and your divorce as the biggest business transaction of your life (it very well may be!).

It is counterproductive to allow yourself to be drawn into emotional arguments and confrontations that are likely to be costly, both financially and emotionally. Know what you want to happen or what kind of financial arrangement you need. This requires that you do a fair amount of homework. You may want to seek the help of a professional financial advisor. Here's a short list of subject matter to get you started.

Monthly expenses. You need to do a post-divorce budget. Draw up a list of how your expenses will be different once your divorce is final. Expenses such as housing and utilities will probably be duplicated. Divide your expenses into non-discretionary and discretionary. This will give a good feel for what your income requirements will be.

Retirement analysis. While you may be focused on your immediate needs, don't overlook the critical long-term issues of retirement. Retirement planning requires complex analysis and multiple assumptions. If you and your spouse have investments in both retirement plans and personal investment plans, would you be better off receiving one or the other in the divorce settlement? What are the tax ramifications of accepting one asset over another?

Debts. Complete a detailed inventory of all family debts, including balances, interest rates, monthly payments and whose name each debt is in. Take precautions to insure that no new debt is incurred before finalizing your divorce. This will often require legal intervention from your lawyer. You want to protect your credit standing, particularly if you have not built a strong credit history on your own. Order your credit report from the credit bureau to determine your current standing.

Saving Your Assets

Children's issues. If you have children, pay particular attention to financial issues, especially any future expenses. Parents often underestimate the costs associated with raising children. Review your bank and credit card statements to estimate what you will spend on your children annually. Take into account fees for after-school activities, camp or braces. If you have a teen, do you provide a car or other big-ticket items? And don't forget about college. The cost of putting a child through the University of Alabama or Auburn can run $10,000 per year or more. Are you thinking about private college? Count on spending $30,000 per year or more. That is just in today's dollars. While general inflation has been very low over the past few years, the costs of funding a college education have been rising at 6% per year.

Asset inventory. You should prepare a detailed inventory of all your family's assets. For financial assets, be sure to include account numbers and the location of accounts as well as account balances. List all items of personal property. Ultimately, these assets will be divided by you or the court as part of the divorce settlement. You should think about which assets are most important to your ultimate financial security into the future. Do you prefer the house or a larger share of the retirement accounts?

Once you complete this exercise, review your needs in light of the family's current financial circumstances. Are your needs realistically going to be agreed upon by either your spouse or the courts? You are likely to find that significant financial adjustments will be necessary. By developing a thorough divorce settlement agreement, you can reduce the likelihood of going back to court in later years, an exercise which is both unpleasant and expensive.

These are just a few of the financial issues. In addition there is an array of non-financial issues you will need to deal with. As you can see, divorce is a complicated emotional and financial event. Once you have determined that divorce is your only course of action, one of the best moves you can make is to hire a lawyer who specializes in divorce work. John Wood and Paul Shaw give you the behind-the-scenes details on how to find and work effectively with a divorce attorney. They cover both the financial aspects as well as the emotional aspects of completing a successful divorce.

-- Stewart H. Welch, III

Stewart H. Welch, III, is founder of The Welch Group, LLC, a fee-only wealth management firm in Birmingham, Alabama. He is the author of two books and co-author of "J.K. Lasser's New Rules for Estate Planning and Taxes" (John Wiley & Sons, Inc.) In addition, he is a financial columnist for The Birmingham Post Herald and contributing editor to Physician's Money Digest. He has been named by Money, Worth, Medical Economics, Bloomberg Wealth Manager and Mutual Funds Magazine as one of the top financial advisors in America.

INTRODUCTION

Your divorce may represent the single most important financial transaction you will ever make. Financial decisions made early in a divorce may impact you for the remainder of your life and should be taken very seriously. Unfortunately, the emotional aspects of divorce are so intertwined with the financial that many people make rash decisions that may seem wise at the time but are later understood to be horrible mistakes.

Saving Your Assets When You Can't Save Your Marriage is intended to help you come to your senses, to snap out of the emotional malaise that overtakes people at the time of divorce. Just like the original book in this series, *The Successful Divorce*, it describes an intelligent approach to the process. It is an approach that takes the various facts, assets, debts and faults of each marriage and factors them into the resolution of your case. The financial ramifications of a divorce on husbands, wives and children can be devastating. Therefore, such a transaction should not be considered lightly or without sound advice from lawyers, financial planners, accountants and counselors.

This book is designed to spur a reality check by those of you who are ending marriages. First we ask you to look at the possibility that, through counseling, you might stay married. Then we give you a realistic appraisal of what your life and lifestyle will look like during and after the divorce. A great number of people, responding emotionally, commit to a settlement and realize too late that they agreed to something that's financially impossible. A fellow attorney once described the perfect negotiation as follows: one party gives too much and the other party takes too little. If you are one of these parties and the negotiation is part of a divorce settlement, it could mean disaster. So proceed with caution and the advice of trained professionals. Divorce is not fair. But with good sound advice you can position yourself to make the wisest decisions possible at such an important time in your life.

This advice goes equally for men and women. This book makes numerous references to the husband and the wife, as well as referencing "she" and "he," the "parents" and the "parties." For purposes of this work, please accept the "he/she" references as being applicable to both parties and not as any kind of gender-based designation. The same goes for references to the attorney. There are many excellent male and female matrimonial lawyers and all references are intended to be applicable to both. This book is primarily based on the statutes and controlling case law for the State of Alabama. The examples used in this book are largely based on prior cases or are composites of people in situations in the Alabama Court System. No references should be construed to indicate that only a wife or only a husband could act in a particular manner. Many husbands have attempted to take financial advantage of their wives in a divorce. Just as many wives have done the same to their husbands. One thing is true of almost all husbands and wives. Each feels terribly taken advantage of by the other after a divorce.

Due to the emotional aspects of each family law case, it is extremely difficult for a divorcing person to be happy afterward. A client of ours once compared the divorce process to having a terrible accident and waking up to find both legs amputated. While you might be happy to be alive, you don't really feel like thanking the doctor for the outcome.

Saving Your Assets

While this material educates you about the financial aspects of divorce, it is not a how-to book. After reading this book, you are not qualified to represent yourself in a divorce. Some other books may prepare you for this, but we don't recommend this course of action. The financial aspects of divorce are so complicated that you need to seek legal counsel along with advice from other professionals.

Saving Your Assets When You Can't Save Your Marriage addresses the financial issues related to a divorce in much greater detail than our original book, *The Successful Divorce*. This book only addresses the issues of child custody and trial preparation as they impact your wallet. Even though we center on the financial aspects of divorce, this material merely serves as an overview of the major financial issues. Each case is based on individual facts and this book should not be used as a replacement for specific legal advice or independent counsel.

-- John M. Wood

-- Paul B. Shaw, Jr.

Wood ◆ Shaw

Divorce Stats

Total divorces granted in the U.S. each year:
1.1 million

State with the lowest divorce rate:
Massachusetts, 2.4 per 1,000 population

State with the highest divorce rate:
Nevada, 9.0 per 1,000 population

Alabama divorce rate:
6.2 per 1,000 population
(seventh highest in the country)

Estimated average length of divorce from start to finish:
1 year

Number of divorced people nationwide:
8.331 million men (8% of total)
11.093 million women (10% of total)

Estimated number of children involved in divorce:
1.075 million

PART ONE

Divorce Planning: Where, When and How to Begin

The next time I think about getting married, instead I'll just find a woman who hates me and buy her a house.

Lewis Grizzard

CHAPTER 1

The Hard Truth
About Money and Divorce

A man who is married for the third time lamented the mathematics of his earlier, and admittedly foolish, years. In pursuit of an elusive state of happiness, this man built up a significant net worth only to see his wealth slashed in half during a divorce. He did that twice and is left in middle age to rebuild his finances once again.

This is the story of many people who've come through the age of divorce, from the 1960s through the early 1980s. According to a survey published in TIME magazine, the average net worth of married couples today, ages 51 to 61, is $132,200. Those who are divorced average only $33,700.[1]

Great attention is paid to the emotional costs of such life choices. *The Unexpected Legacy of Divorce*, therapist Judith Wallerstein's 25-year landmark study of 131 children of divorce, centers on the painful search of these "lost" children, now adults, who are struggling to overcome the feeling that love and trust are doomed. Far too little notice has been paid to the devastating financial impact divorce imposes on divorcing people and their children, as well as their extended families. High emotions create financial woes, which generate more emotional upheaval. Before you make the decision to divorce, give yourself a reality check to see if that's really what you want.

Most people facing the financial realities of divorce reach this point with mixed feelings about their situation. Some people are astounded at the amount of money they have accumulated during the marriage. Add the equity in a house to the total of their personal property, the amount in retirement funds and perhaps the value of a business and a seemingly middle class family can be worth several million dollars.

Others are stunned at how little their union was worth. Living in a large home, driving new cars, sending their kids to the best private schools and vacationing at the beach in summer and the mountains during ski season took every penny they earned. These couples are left with only debts.

Few people are unaffected by the money pit that divorce can become. In most cases, that is true for both the payor spouse and the recipient spouse. The payor spouse is the one who usually winds up with more of the assets or a business, for whatever reason, and must pay child support and alimony to a recipient spouse. For the payor spouse, the payments can be devastating. For the recipient spouse, the total payment rarely equals the pre-divorce living allowance. This money once paid for a single household. Now the parties expect the same amount of money to pay for two homes. No court order or act of God can make the money stretch far enough to afford the same lifestyle enjoyed before the divorce.

Imagine doubling every expense in your monthly household budget — two house payments, two gas bills, two power bills and two grocery bills—and attempting to pay these bills with the same combined monthly income. Very few families can shoulder this burden and maintain the same lifestyle without serious deficit spending. Both spouses feel entitled to the savings account, the retirement plan and the equity in the home. And neither lays claim to the debt.

The emotional and financial aspects of divorce are inter-twined so completely that otherwise fiscally savvy people often become their own worst enemy by the way they resolve their divorce. Some want to get the divorce over quickly. This desire clouds all logic and causes one spouse to accept a poor settlement in an effort to bring closure. Bringing a swift end to the marriage, however, often leaves at least one of the spouses with a financially insecure future.

On the other hand, you may be so consumed with the need for revenge that you'd rather give all your money to lawyers and other professionals than let that no-good ex of yours have pocket change to spend when the divorce is over.

Many people have a common misconception that the divorce process will work itself out in a way that is financially fair. If you remember anything from this book, know that the law is not suf-ficiently designed to always make things fair. The court can only divide assets according to the law and the evidence, and that does not always result in fairness. To survive the financial impact of a divorce, determine your needs and the options you have for meeting those needs. Even if you are still deciding whether to divorce, or are not certain your spouse is about to file, this kind of planning is essential.

A thorough examination of your financial standing, along with an exhaustive review of budgets and needs, will help you map out the most successful financial outcome possible. Only after an in-depth study has been made of all income sources, expenses, assets and liabilities can an accurate analysis suggest a division of assets and debts in the divorce. Most of the time, spouses find after this analysis that divorce is not fair. The law requires only equitably apportioning the assets and debts among the parties.

It's constantly surprising how little the average person knows about divorce in Alabama. Even people who've been divorced two or three times know few of the nuances of a successful financial divorce.

**The financial strain of divorce
may make it impossible
to get back on your feet.
Get your thoughts together
to protect your financial interests.**

A Former Client

Nine Basic Truths
of an Alabama Divorce

It's your divorce, but Alabama law controls it. There is a set of truths common to every case, including the following:

Truth #1: There will be a 30-day waiting period from the time you file the divorce until it can be final, even with an uncontested divorce.

Truth #2: Once a divorce is filed and one party wants to go through with it, you can't stop it from happening.

Truth #3: Contentious, litigated divorces are more financially devastating than agreed settlements.

Truth #4: All property must be divided equitably, which may be different from "equally."

Truth #5: The spouse who does not have primary custody of the children will, in almost every case, pay child support.

Truth #6: If the other side requests your financial information, you will have to comply unless you settle. Even then, the other side may not settle without getting the information.

Truth #7: Your spouse can still file bankruptcy after the divorce, leaving you with the responsibility for certain debts.

Truth #8: It is difficult to reopen a case later. With only one bite at the apple, specify everything you want from the property settlement.

Truth #9: Your divorce is not final until the court enters the order. So you cannot "act single" until you are.

"When you feel a lot of anxiety, you can be tempted to make a quick decision. If you can hang in there, the odds increase that eventually you will make the choice that is best for you at the time."

Counselor Nancy Wasson, Ph.D.

CHAPTER 2

Is Divorce the Answer?

It's not news that divorce can be a bad thing for parents and children. But many recent books – both clinical studies like Judith Wallerstein's *The Unexpected Legacy of Divorce* and memoirs like Stephanie Stahl's *The Love They Lost: Living with the Legacy of Our Parents' Divorce* – consider divorce such a harsh remedy that they suggest people stay together even when they can't stand each other.

No Short-Term Fix

The controversial notion that people should stay together for the children is a throwback to the 1950s and before, when divorce was rare. After so many divorces over the past three decades, we realize that divorce is not a short-term fix for marital problems. It is emotionally draining with the potential to be the worst experience of your entire life. Further, it may create more problems than the marriage, especially as it relates to financial matters. Ensure that you are prepared for the process and aware of the opportunities to save your marriage. Before proceeding with a divorce, exhaust every available avenue to avoid it. Each community has a network of religious advisors, marriage counselors and support groups. Discuss your uncertainty with close friends. If you have children, talk to divorced parents to determine the pros and cons of their situations. Remember that "the grass is always greener on the other side of the fence" and you may be looking at an optical illusion.

Licensed professional counselor Nancy Wasson suggests that big life decisions, such as whether to stay married or divorce, need to be made when you are feeling calm and centered, after you have taken as much time as you need to explore the options.

Situations that involve abusive, violent or other unacceptable behavior fall into another category entirely. When there isn't time to seek legal advice, a decision must be made immediately for your safety and the safety of your children. Once that decision has been made, you should get sound legal advice and utilize the justice system to prevent further deterioration of the situation.

But a relationship doesn't have to be abusive to be emotionally and financial damaging. In the 1970s and early 80s, the percentage of first-time marriages that resulted in divorce peaked at about 65 percent.[2] It is fortunate for all of society that those percentages have fallen over the past decade. Still, about 40 percent of first marriages end in divorce.[3] That's a lot of anger and confusion, both emotionally and financially. When people feel that way, few things are more cathartic than making a decision. At some point you may have to stop the discussion, settle things once and for all and file for divorce.

For most people, making that decision is scary but liberating. You've thought about the downside. You know money will be tight. Taking care of your family will be more difficult. And having to sift through the financial details of your life with this person will not be fun.

But by making the decision, you are taking your fate into your own hands and that is empowering.

The Decision is Made

Divorce planning is a whole new occupation that centers on smoothing over financial bumps at the end of marriage. You may be more familiar with the job of the wedding planner, who fusses over details of how many ushers and bridesmaids to outfit, what kind of groom's cake to order and where to place flowers in the chapel. The work of the divorce planner is certainly not as romantic, but it is equally important to the continued happiness of the parties.

Certified divorce planner Mary Wier [4] instructs divorcing people to collect financial information and organize it before seeing your attorney. In fact, you should even begin your planning and organization before your spouse knows you intend to file for divorce.

This is one of the more controversial aspects of divorce planning. How aggressively you plan your escape is always subject to debate. Many people feel that taking several months or a year to plan your departure is simply too cold-blooded, cuts off attempts to save your marriage too early and can alienate those around you. There is a difference between planning and taking calculated steps to hide or dispose of assets. Planning is good, but the other may come back to haunt you at trial. Still, if you move into divorce with little forethought, you may be setting yourself up for a life-long disaster. Considering the dire consequences of inaction, assertive action will help you achieve the successful financial divorce.

Certified divorce planner Mary Wier offers a list of "do's and don't's" for people facing the financial aspects of divorce. Among these are:

<u>DO</u> look at the long-term financial effects of the proposed settlement.

<u>DO</u> be reasonable in your expectations, not expecting your spouse to be punished or for you to be rewarded.

<u>DO</u> try to work out personal property issues with your spouse instead of submitting the asset division to the judge. He or she won't know the personal significance of your property.

<u>DON'T</u> sign any agreements without reading and understanding them first.

<u>DON'T</u> count on alimony to support your lifestyle or, in the case of the payor spouse, to hinder it.

<u>DON'T</u> forget the tax man!

<u>DON'T</u> hesitate to hire trained experts to assist you.

Prenuptial Agreements

For those who plan for the possibility of disaster, premarital agreements or "prenups" are a perfectly reasonable response. Prenuptial agreements are most popular with people who enter a marriage with large assets and want to preserve them in case of a divorce. Some of are not easily divisible, such as an interest in a family owned business or a large tract of real estate. Keeping them intact is a prime reason for the prenup.

This type of agreement is a financial contract between the parties. It works like any other partnership agreement and should be crafted with an understanding of the couple's overall financial situation, including:

- The couple's financial condition
- Assets to be protected
- Who earns the income in the marriage and how
- How expenses of the marriage will be paid
- Protecting separate assets as circumstances change
- Changes in income during the marriage
- How to record amounts due under the agreement
- How the agreement will affect future financial decisions
- Allocation of debts during the marriage

For the other party to the marriage, reversing the terms or "breaking" a well written prenup can be difficult. Only when the prenuptial agreement is poorly written can a property settlement become difficult to enforce and add uncertainty that would not exist without an agreement.

Prenuptial agreements have gotten so much press lately that even people with modest holdings sometimes draw up papers so that a split can be less messy.

Enforcing Your Prenup

In Alabama, two tests are important when attempting to enforce a prenuptial agreement. The agreement must meet one or the other (but not necessarily both) to be enforceable:

That the consideration was adequate and the entire transaction was fair, just and equitable from the other party's point of view; OR

That the agreement was entered into freely and voluntarily by the other party, with competent, independent legal advice and full knowledge of that party's interest in the estate and its approximate value.

Socking Away Information

Most married couples include what you might call a "documented" spouse and an "undocumented" one. The documented spouse usually makes most of the money, pays the bills and maintains the records. The undocumented spouse has little to do with family finances. That spouse is at a distinct disadvantage at the beginning of a divorce case.

It is much easier
to gather the financial
information while the
marriage is working
than after the divorce
is filed and everyone
is suspicious of
each other.

Saving Your Assets

Never allow yourself to be the undocumented spouse. Think of yourself as an information magnet in the early days of your divorce. Information can make or break your case at trial. Insist on being a partner in the process of paying bills. You have to secure that information so your spouse won't spring it on you at trial or make it hard to obtain.

The most relevant items include three to five years of the following:

- Personal or corporate tax returns
- Checking, savings and money market account statements
- Paid bills
- Investment account statements
- Stock or bond certificates
- Mortgage information
- Credit card information
- Information on debts and other liabilities
- Long-distance telephone bills
- Cellular telephone bills
- Medical records
- Health insurance policies
- Life insurance policies
- Photo evidence of extramarital affairs
- Any other evidence that establishes fault by the other side

Put this information away for safekeeping. It might be pertinent if used at trial, and it might not. But you want the opportunity to make that decision by having it available.

Obtaining this information does not assure you of winning

most of the marital assets in a divorce. The facts of your case will dictate whether you can use this information. It should be available to you for reasons other than divorce, such as your spouse's death or illness. With your family's financial information in hand, you can exert more control and know what is at stake.

Hiding Money, Tracing Assets

Bank account records reveal crucial information. Often they contain facts and figures known by only one of the marriage partners. For example, most people get paid twice a month, so the account would include deposits to a checking account, customarily, on the first and 15th of each month. What if your spouse claims a monthly income of $10,000 but deposits $25,000 into the checking account each month? This may indicate large commissions or bonuses. You need to know the source of that income, how it is being used and how you can get your hands on it.

In one case, we suspected the husband was hiding money but couldn't prove it. Everything looked clean, maybe too clean. After much searching, we were looking at cancelled checks and happened to notice where they were deposited. An account number on the back of one check didn't ring any bells. When we checked our list of accounts, the account wasn't on the list. A trickle of money turned into a torrent when we issued a subpoena for the records of that account. In this way, we discovered a separate set of books and a lot of hidden money.

Asset tracing is a delicate skill involving advanced investigation techniques. But anyone who can read a bank statement can do some of this.

Spying, Sneaking and Snooping Can Uncover the Truth

Information obtained through investigation can become devastatingly effective pieces of evidence. Long-distance and cellular telephone records are great examples. Just after your spouse has told the judge that he or she does not know a certain person of the opposite sex, you bring forth an enlarged phone statement with page after page of cellular calls to that person's number.

The best divorce lawyers will request both personal and business cellular phone and long-distance records for the past three to five years. If a spouse has been hiding these calls behind business accounts, the information will prove valuable and the guilty spouse could settle the case to keep an employer from finding out about those extracurricular activities.

Catching your spouse "red handed" is effective. But too often, people operate on a hunch, suspecting something without being able to prove it. Spying and snooping without justification can wreck an already weak marriage.

Take the offensive and get the best agreement you can while your spouse is being apologetic. Once time has passed, the willingness to do *the right thing* may change.

Proof is the divider between whether your information is effective or not. If you can't prove it, your information doesn't really exist and shouldn't be used in court. Presenting potentially damaging information without solid proof just makes you look vindictive and deceitful. The decision whether to present certain evidence is not an easy one to make. This decision has to be made in the context of the overall strategy of your case.

Split Decisions 5

If you see a divorce coming in your life, you'll need to batten down your financial hatches. Here's what divorce lawyers and financial planners suggest:

Make A List

Prepare a list of the family's assets and liabilities. Know where to find financial documents.

Save

Start saving money in your own separate bank account, so you'll have cash to pay bills. Be careful not to be perceived as hiding money.

Divvy it Up

Decide which assets you would like to keep and which you're willing to give up.

Pare it Down

Don't expect the same lifestyle you did when you were married. Divorce can be financially devastating to both partners.

Get Credit

Apply for credit in your own name so you can start building an individual credit history.

Know the Law

Know divorce law for your state. Alabama provides for an equitable division of assets from a marriage. That doesn't mean a court will divide assets 50-50.

Wood ◆ Shaw

To be prepared for
War is one of the
most effectual means
of preserving peace.

George Washington

CHAPTER 3

Uncontested Divorce Or Nuclear War?

Norene assumed the divorce would not be contested. She knew exactly what property she wanted from the marriage. It didn't matter what her husband, Greg, wanted. He had always been the passive one in the relationship. There was no reason to believe the divorce would be any different.

So when Norene went to see her lawyer, she wanted to know the fee for an uncontested divorce. "All we need is a lawyer to prepare the papers," she told him.

A truly uncontested divorce is the rarest of commodities. It means that people who agree on very little in a marriage — to the point of pulling the plug on the whole thing — will come together and agree on everything involved in saying goodbye.

In the case of Norene and Greg, like many others, the divorce started out cordial enough. Then Greg talked to his buddies and soon he was speaking up like never before. Ego, pride, jealousy, rage and resentment intermingled with substantive property issues. Someone said something that shouldn't have been said, and that earlier spirit of agreement was destroyed. An uncontested divorce suddenly became both contested and expensive.

How Wide the War?

If you want to keep the conflict to a small skirmish, restrain yourself. Keep your mouth shut and stick to the business of divorce. Many agreements that are perfectly fair to both parties collapse after one spouse says something awful to the other before the papers are executed. There are good reasons to nullify agreements, but pride and ego are not among them.

Some people feel that it's civil and smart to have one attorney represent both parties. It may be civil, but it's certainly not smart. An attorney can represent only one party in a divorce. That attorney is protecting the interests of one client, and the other party's rights can be greatly affected by the terms of any settlement agreement entered into between the parties.

If your spouse insists on having just one attorney, make sure the attorney is representing you. Without that protection, prepare yourself for a disaster that could affect you the rest of your life.

Keeping Your Spouse As a Friend

How important is it for you to remain on speaking terms with your soon-to-be ex spouse? In consultation with an attorney, decide just how much that friendship is worth. How much are you willing to concede to keep the other side happy?

At a time like this, when you are your most vulnerable, the steady hand of an emotionally disinterested party who is experienced at handling divorce matters may keep you from making the mistake of a lifetime.

If you want to keep the divorce uncontested, do yourself a favor. Have a matrimonial law expert simply assess your situation, inform you of your rights and advise you about various scenarios that might save you trouble in the long run.

When Your Spouse Becomes the Enemy

There comes a time in many divorces when communication breaks down and progress grinds to a halt. This is when a divorce becomes contested and difficult. Often this point comes when you least suspect it, in the midst of negotiations that are meant to end the struggle but just create more emotion and heat.

To ready yourself, remember that your spouse, regrettably, is now the enemy, if just for the duration of the divorce. After all, this person wants to keep assets you need to pay bills. This may sound cutthroat, but it is true. Of course, you may need to temper that if young children are involved. After all, your spouse will be your child's parent for the rest of his or her life.

Planning Your Divorce Strategy

"Peace through strength" was a maxim of our national policy during the Cold War. The same goes for your approach to a divorce strategy. All contested divorces should be handled as though you were certain they could wind up in trial. Then if you

Sometimes Fault Breaks a Tie

In an Alabama divorce, the judge can consider the fault of the parties in the division of assets and debts. Types of fault considered by the judge may include:

- Adultery
- Drug use
- Alcoholism
- Physical abuse of a spouse or child
- Mental abuse of a spouse or child
- Sexual abuse of a spouse or child
- Overly suspicious or obsessive behavior
- Gambling
- Excessive spending
- Mental illness or psychological problems
- Criminal convictions
- Unusual sexual practices
- Long absences from home

Whatever the fault is, you have to prove it. The courts often utilize what is called the "reasonable person's standard." The judge considers whether the evidence indicates the behavior of a married person properly executing family duties. Most people in successful marriages are not seen frequently in bars late at night with a person of the opposite sex. They usually pay their house payment before gambling at the racetrack. And they don't disappear from home for days at a time.

can settle things, you are ahead of the game. If settlement efforts fail, you are prepared for the battle. Sometimes a little "sabre rattling" must be done so the other side knows you are serious.

Alternative Dispute Resolution

Let the litigation battle commence! That should have been the battle cry when Bob and Irene Vargas decided to divorce. No two people ever disagreed as much, even over the most trivial details. Although Bob was in the printing business, they couldn't even agree that some antique books and magazines rightfully belonged to him.

The Vargases' attorneys saw their ability to battle firsthand. During their only settlement conference, the two of them stood across the table like rhinos about to charge, bellowing at each other. Since that meeting, their attorneys engaged in telephone tag, with Bob calling his attorney, who called Irene's attorney, who called Irene, but she was out, so she had to call back. Then Irene's attorney called Bob's attorney, who called Bob. Then Bob realized he was "it." He had another question, and the whole process started all over again.

With the meter running on both sides, the attorneys' bills were ballooning and still they hadn't gone to trial. Soon neither side would have any money left.

Growing Importance of Mediation

Also known as alternative dispute resolution or assisted negotiation, mediation was conceived for people such as Bob and Irene. It involves communication and compromise triumphing over conflict. That's especially crucial for people who will have to continue a financial relationship, such as the owners of a family business or a couple who agrees to long-term alimony.

Explaining the Process

Moving the process from the courthouse to the mediator's office often reduces the adversarial tension inherent in a divorce. The job of a divorce lawyer in court is to present the facts in a light most favorable to the client and win most of the assets. The job of a divorce lawyer in mediation is to negotiate the best deal for the client, in light of the facts that would be presented at trial, within the context of an agreement that will hold up over time.

In most cases, the actual mediation process begins with the parties and their representatives — attorneys, accountants, financial planners or brokers — meeting in the same room. Here the mediator lays out the ground rules in 15 to 30 minutes of expla-

---

The mediation process has become more popular over the past decade. In most cases, it's less expensive to mediate than litigate.

nation. Then the parties are separated and the mediator begins a day of shuttle diplomacy, moving from room to room highlighting points of agreement, attempting to smooth over disagreements and helping the parties come up with creative ways to resolve the case.

The best mediators are very effective at getting people to look toward common goals over the long term. Once an agreement is reached, a mediated settlement agreement is prepared and signed by the parties and their attorneys. From this document, the attorneys draft a Final Judgment of Divorce, which is signed by the judge, and the divorce is complete.

Mediation is the single most significant change in family law in the past 25 years. Of about 2,240 family courts in this country, perhaps 200 offer (sometimes require) mediation in some cases. [6] The overcrowding of court dockets and a rising concern that making divorce an adversarial process is not in the best interest of children have prompted this change from litigation to mediation.

One mediation practice reports that for mediated divorces over an 11-year period, 92 percent were settled and didn't go to court. Of those mediated settlements, 89 percent still remain in force. [7]

Beware of Mediation Abusers

Critics of the mediation process often ask how you reach a fair settlement when one side is hiding money or purposely devaluing assets for the property division. Mediation under these circumstances can be very difficult. Going through the discovery process of accounts and assets prior to mediation can lessen the danger of an unfair settlement. Generally, undertaking mediation without receiving sworn discovery responses about financial matters from your spouse is risky. But we've seen clients go into mediation skeptical of the other side's motives and still come out with a worthwhile agreement.

Wood ◆ Shaw

What qualities does your divorce attorney need to possess? Some are wizards at tracing hidden assets. Some skillfully handle aggressive acts from the other side. Others are masters of effective settlement.

CHAPTER 4

Hiring Expert Help

Your Family Lawyer

Unfortunately, the point at which a divorce takes place is the best possible time to be skeptical of other peoples' motives. When we are brought into a case to clean up an existing mess, it is often because someone trusted too much. In matters of love, a little cynicism seems to go a long way. Most of the problems of divorcing people come from misplaced trust.

There is the client who agreed with her husband that their divorce should be simple, inexpensive and civil. She worked out the division of property with her husband, an older man and experienced businessperson. And after the couple agreed on a settlement, they submitted it all to the attorney he used to handle business disputes for his small trucking company. The husband provided the attorney with a valuation of his business along with

Saving Your Assets

the specific details of all their bank accounts and investments.

The woman felt comfortable with the attorney, who had been a guest in their home several times. But during the process she discovered – quite by accident – a bank account her husband failed to disclose. When we entered the case, we ordered a business valuation along with details of the missing account. The original value given the business was incredibly low. All in all, the man tried to cheat his wife out of several hundred thousand dollars. Luckily, the divorce was not final and we were able to get the woman what she deserved. But trusting her former partner almost did her in.

Can you trust your soon-to-be ex-spouse to be truthful? And can you get accurate answers from an attorney you did not hire? If you want to emerge financially intact, don't do either. If you are going to be involved in a divorce, hire a matrimonial law expert who is prepared and capable to handle your case. The law has become very specialized over the past few decades and most attorneys now concentrate in one or two practice areas. The same principles you utilize in selecting a physician can be employed to choose a lawyer. If you are diagnosed with cancer, you want the best cancer doctor around. The same applies to your divorce. If you are going to have a litigated asset trial, you need a matrimonial law expert. Likewise, if you have your own business or large assets, you need to hire a firm with the capabilities and staff to manage a large asset case.

Whatever your need, there is an attorney who can help you with it. There are more than one million licensed attorneys in the United States, more than 11,000 in Alabama alone. One of the best ways to locate the correct attorney for you is to ask divorced people whom they recommend. You may know an attorney who practices in a field other than matrimonial law. Ask that attorney to refer you to a good family lawyer. Your local bar association may have a referral service. Marriage counselors, accountants, financial planners, business managers and clergy often know family lawyers with outstanding reputations and good track records.

Initial Interviews

There may be many attorneys in your town with the legal ability to do the job. Isolate at least two of them and schedule initial interviews. What you're looking for is the qualified attorney who best suits your personality. Chances are you will be working in close proximity with this person for a year to 18 months. Life is too short to spend that time with someone you personally dislike.

A short interview with each of the qualified candidates will tell you which attorney works best with you. Each attorney you speak with will want to cover the basic history of the marriage and the issues involved in the divorce. Be as candid as possible, letting the attorney know all your good points and all your faults. Lawyers are under an ethical obligation not to disclose to anyone the information you provide, unless you consent to the disclosure. In addition, the following items are very helpful for the lawyer to know at the initial meeting:

- Length of the marriage
- Names and ages of children and any special needs
- Fault of the husband
- Fault of the wife

- Child care by each party
- Income of each party
- Work history of each party
- List of assets (Figure 3)
- List of debts (Figure 4)

The lawyer may ask you to prepare a detailed timeline and summary of the marital history after the initial interview. It is important that you be extremely honest and completely forthcoming in providing this information. The lawyer needs to know each and every issue that your spouse could bring up during the case. It is impossible to get a correct evaluation of your case unless you present the lawyer with all the facts on both sides and ask the right questions.

Questions to Ask the Lawyer

"Do you charge for the initial interview?"

Most matrimonial lawyers charge for the initial visit, while some attorneys offer a free consultation. This fee can range from $100 to several hundred dollars. Our firm charges an initial consultation fee because of the time necessary to conduct a thorough initial interview.

Also, the initial interview creates a conflict for the lawyer. Once an attorney meets with one spouse and hears the marital history, he or she cannot represent the other spouse. In most cases, if you hire the attorney the initial interview charge is paid from the retainer.

"How do you charge for your services?"

Most matrimonial lawyers bill on an hourly basis for work performed by the lawyers and paralegals in the firm, while a flat fee may be charged for certain limited services. Become a smart consumer of legal services and choose the attorney who can meet your expectations at a price you can afford. Matrimonial attorneys in Alabama typically charge from $100 per hour to $300 per hour or more, depending on location and credentials. A highly experienced matrimonial law attorney with a track record of outstanding representation, handling a complex case in one of the state's largest cities, can use a significant amount of time and bill thousands of dollars. Expect to be billed every time you meet with the lawyer, call him or her on the telephone or ask the office staff to work on your case.

You should have a clear understanding how the lawyer bills. The litigation budget discussed in Chapter 8 will help you estimate your potential expenses.

"Do I sign a fee agreement?"

Most lawyers will have you execute a written fee agreement when you decide to retain him or her. Review the agreement and understand how you will be billed — whether by flat fee or against a retainer — and what other expenses you are obligated to pay. Determine the initial fee and when it must be paid. A flat fee is a lump sum, one-time payment for handling the entire case. A retainer is an advance payment the lawyer uses to pay his bills for time and expenses.

Retainers must be refundable under Alabama State Bar rules. For example, say you give the attorney a $5,000 retainer. The attorney does $3,000 worth of legal work on your case, but then you decide to reconcile with your spouse or come to the conclusion that this attorney is not the right one for you. The attorney is required to refund the remaining $2,000.

The fee agreement should also address supplemental retainers throughout the case. The initial retainer may not get you through the entire case. If it is a large asset or hotly litigated case, you may be required to supplement your retainer several times during the process.

The agreement should also specify what expenses you are obligated to pay, such as long distance charges, subpoena fees, photocopy and fax charges. The fee agreement may also address the possibility of your spouse being required by the court to pay your fees and how that payment would be applied.

Your lawyer cannot pinpoint exactly how much your case will cost before the case begins. The actions of your spouse, the opposing attorney or others involved in the case determine that. At the same time, the lawyer should be able to give you a potential range of fees based on the issues involved.

The tremendous expense involved in litigating a divorce with many financial components may shock you. Your fees could range from several thousand dollars to a hundred thousand dollars or more, depending upon the assets and issues involved.

"Who is my contact in the firm?"

During the initial interview, determine which attorneys and

staff members will work on your case. Some firms have one lawyer and one receptionist, so the number of contact points is limited. Many other matrimonial law firms have several lawyers, paralegals, secretaries and other professionals, including office managers, private investigators and affiliated experts. It is helpful for the client to have several points of contact within the firm so that if a problem arises and the lawyer handling the case is in court or unavailable, you can speak to someone familiar with your case. At our firm, we assign at least one attorney and one paralegal to each case. In addition, lawyers meet each week to discuss the firm's cases. If a client calls and the lawyer or paralegal assigned primary responsibility for that case is out of the office, other members of the firm must be prepared to address emergencies until the primary attorney returns.

Many large asset cases require the attention of two or more lawyers. For example, one lawyer may concentrate on the marriage history facts and the witnesses while another lawyer works specifically on assets and business accounting issues related to the case. It is enough for one attorney to know the history of a 20-year marriage with three children and a spouse with a drinking problem. The other attorney concentrates on the financial terms, conditions and history of a successful multimillion dollar business, along with the details of the purchase and acquisition of all assets and debts of the marriage.

If your case involves significant assets, debts or other complications, make certain the lawyer you hire has the necessary experience and time to prepare your case. You know everything about your case because you have been living it. But you must bring your lawyer up to speed so that he or she may try the case

and explain all the details to the judge. This is an extremely difficult process. The lawyer must balance the time he believes the
court will allow to try the case against the client's emotions and
the details the client feels are critically important.

Most clients get upset with attorneys who won't return
phone calls or give their cases the attention they demand. In most
instances, you get what you pay for. If you have a large asset case
that may be litigated over a year or more, it will be difficult for the
lawyer to charge you a minimal flat fee. If he or she does that, ask
yourself if that fee will adequately cover the necessary time. If the
cost is too good to be true, it just might be, and attention to your
case could wane.

"Do you send out monthly statements?"

Constantly monitor the charges incurred in your case on a
regular basis. Lawyers and staff members must do a lot of work
to prepare your case for trial. Even if you are not talking to the
lawyer on a regular basis, work is probably being done on your
behalf.

Use your lawyer's time wisely. If you call the lawyer daily and
use the law firm as an emotional counseling service, your bill will
increase dramatically. At most firms, attorneys and paralegals
record their time each day. Monthly statements inform the client
about the status of the case as well as billing charges incurred to
date. We ask clients to review our statements and call with any
questions to avoid surprises or confusion at the end of the case.
You do not want to wait until the end of a yearlong case to find
out your balance is several times your estimated budget.

"How long will my case take?"

A divorce that settles is generally resolved faster than one that is litigated. A large asset or hotly litigated case could easily take a year to 18 months to resolve. Some cases take longer than two years to resolve due to the intricacies and delays. If you are headed toward litigation, you can count on a year or more of preparation and delay until you have your divorce. Delays are due to the large number of divorce cases in the court system as well as the effort required to determine the individual assets and other issues involved.

If your spouse fails to provide financial records without a subpoena, your case will take longer to resolve than if both sides put all the information on the table. If you must provide audits and detailed financial examinations of the assets and values of the businesses involved, take into account the scheduling and availability of other professionals.

If your spouse or your spouse's lawyer decides to be difficult and battle every facet of the case, your divorce will take longer and become a great deal more expensive than if the parties resolve the case through settlement. Most cases start out litigated while tempers and emotions run very high. But time and mounting fees have a magical way of calming those emotions and allowing the parties to settle.

We try to determine the assets, debts and faults of the marriage and proceed down the path of settlement in each case. Some cases, though, are easier to litigate than to settle because the other side won't allow them to settle. At some point, a decision must be made whether to continue settlement negotiations or simply try the case. Only a few cases are easier to try. But sometimes having the judge make a ruling resolves the case more quickly and reasonably than expecting the parties to resolve their differences.

"What do you expect of your client?"

Get a sense of how much cooperation the lawyer expects from you. We generally expect each client to do a great deal of homework. This homework usually involves the client obtaining or developing information to help us fully understand the case. Fee agreements often explain that the client's cooperation is critical. Many firms reserve the right to withdraw from a case if the client will not help the lawyer obtain information they cannot get themselves or if the client is not honest with them. While it's not necessary to communicate with the lawyer every day, it is in your best interest to provide the requested information in a timely fashion. If the lawyer calls to schedule an appointment or obtain additional information, return the call as soon as possible. You should care about the outcome of your divorce at least as much as your attorney.

Dedicate a certain amount of time on a regular basis to help your lawyer prepare. In our experience, a client who is thoroughly involved in the preparation and details of the case is more informed and always happier with the end result.

Wood ◆ Shaw

The spouse who
takes no precautions
before filing and allows
the other spouse to tie
up the money may be
left with little or no
resources.

CHAPTER 5

An Early Look at Finances

Once you are armed with volumes of financial information and teamed with an expert in family law, consider preliminary financial issues and how finances will be managed during the early stages of separation. Before filing the case, assess the options available for financial support in the event the case becomes adversarial. You and your lawyer should also address plans to protect liquid assets and prevent their removal or disposal. Once you have handled these matters, the initial stresses of divorce can be reduced.

A Short-Term Financial Plan

The emotional and financial aspects of divorce hit you in waves at the beginning of the process. First come the court filings.

Then an answer is filed. And after that comes retaliation from the other side. That's how things go the first weeks of almost every case.

Retaliation is most often financial. One spouse can retaliate by refusing to give the other money to pay bills, denying access to certain accounts or charge cards or even selling or hiding certain assets. These actions generally backfire on the offending spouse when the case gets to trial. But the fury of the storm often sends events out of control. If the money is gone or cannot be found, it may be impossible to replace. Months into a divorce, many clients are more concerned about about putting food on the table than resolving the case. As a result, clients must develop a short-term financial plan to protect themselves if the storm surge of financial retaliation overtakes them.

The first step is to determine what income options are available during the first three months after separation. One lawyer or the other will often file a motion for temporary relief, but the court may not be able to schedule that motion for several months. In the meantime, bills and expenses continue to mount on one side, while the potential to misuse assets grows on the other. If one party to the divorce is not working and the other spouse has all the income, additional planning may be necessary.

The spouse with less income needs to develop a safety net if the other spouse attempts to cut off financial assistance. These safety net resources may come from savings accounts, assistance from family members or friends or even short-term loans. This is an area to examine very closely with your attorney before proceeding with a divorce.

If you remove funds from a joint account or take an advance

on a joint credit card, the other side may retaliate by freezing those funds. To avoid this dual problem, initial planning is essential, considering the possible options and consequences of each action. If you utilize joint funds, maintain a clear accounting of how the funds are used. The court usually understands when you use joint funds for groceries and other living expenses. Judges tend to frown on the purchase of jewelry or trips to Aruba.

A woman hired our firm after her husband removed the $750,000 balance from their savings account and claimed he lost the money investing overseas. Once the money was gone, it was virtually impossible to get back. So we went after and won a larger share of the remaining assets. This client will tell you today that she trusted her spouse and did not imagine he would remove the funds. But you cannot spend trust on yourself or your children. She was left in a very vulnerable position due to her failure to anticipate her spouse's actions.

Temporary Restraining Orders

If your case involves large assets titled in the name of your spouse, the best way to protect those assets is by seeking a temporary restraining order (TRO). Certain Alabama courts automatically enter joint restraining orders preventing either party from disposing of assets, while you have to ask for a TRO in others. This can be an expensive procedure that is required on a case-by-case basis. The restraining order simply directs the spouse not to dispose of assets. It does not erect a force field around the assets to prevent their disposal. It is the same as a physical restraining order that attempts to protect a person from harm. While the party violating the order faces possibly severe consequences, the assets can still be removed and you must keep a close eye on them. If you are concerned about the possible disposal or secreting of assets by the other side, address this issue with your lawyer before taking any action.

Who Pays the Bills Initially?

Events happen so slowly in the court system that temporary matters may seem like they go on forever. That's why you should figure out how to pay bills and expenses before filing for divorce. Your lawyer can file a motion for temporary relief and address the bills, child support, possession of the house and other related issues. But the court may not hear those issues for several months as ongoing bills continue to pile up.

Your first concern should be the bills in your name. These may include credit cards and other debts, as well as expenses incurred on behalf of the children, such as extracurricular activities. In an ideal situation, the parties will handle financial matters as they did before the separation. Neither party should incur unreasonably large charges or refuse to pay ordinary expenses customarily paid during the marriage. If your spouse retaliates and refuses to pay certain bills, be sure to pay the bills that are in your name. Make a minimum payment on these accounts to minimize your expenses and protect your credit history. Sometimes a spouse refuses to pay any of the bills, causing the mortgage and other debt obligations to go into default. If this situation arises in your case, ask the court to intervene with a temporary hearing that addresses these matters prior to default.

One of the most effective ways your spouse can exert settlement pressure is to cause you financial stress. If you have already developed a financial plan, you will be much more prepared to deal with the emotional aspects and weather the storm until you can get relief from the court. And keep your plan to yourself. Do not reveal it to your spouse or it may be sabotaged.

If you are the party in the dominant financial position, your actions during this delicate period can have a great impact on later decisions of the trial court. Perhaps you should continue to make the mortgage payment instead of expecting a spouse who does not work to assume responsibility for the payment immediately. Some lawyers advise their clients to discontinue paying private school tuition or mortgage payments they've paid for years. Those spouses may have left their homes and the children in them. But compounding the emotional difficulties related to divorce by refusing to pay the children's expenses does not win praise from the court.

If one party has committed serious fault, such as an adulterous relationship or substance abuse, he or she may reduce the impact of that fault by acting maturely and responsibly during this initial period. If that person makes the debt payments and agrees without court intervention to pay child support and temporary support, it is much easier to show that party in a favorable light. But if one party has left the marriage for another person, cut off all financial support and refused to pay the outstanding bills, there should be no surprise when the judge deals harshly with that party at a final hearing. It is not *that* you left but *how* you left that gets you into trouble.

While trying to settle the case, each party's actions impact the likelihood of settlement. Under normal circumstances, you may have difficulty accepting the idea of settlement. If during that same time your spouse is playing games with the finances – allowing the mortgage to go into default, refusing to pay for summer camp and cutting off credit cards – that case generally moves from the possibility of settlement to nuclear war.

Joint Accounts/Joint Debts

Special attention must be given to joint checking and savings accounts, as well as joint debts. In a perfect world, you and your spouse would maintain these accounts the same as before during the pendency of the case. Be aware that you have legal obligations and liabilities in connection with these accounts.

Under the terms of a joint checking, savings or brokerage account, you or your spouse may be allowed to withdraw all the proceeds of that account.

If you have just deposited your entire paycheck in the account and your spouse empties it, you may be left with no money to pay your bills. If it is a joint credit card account and your spouse continues to incur significant charges on that account, you will be obligated by the creditor for that debt until your name is removed or the court orders otherwise. If you have joint accounts or joint credit cards, immediately consult your lawyer about these accounts.

The court will look at how the accounts were managed prior to the separation. It is also helpful to obtain the last three years' statements to show your attorney and the court the prior use and history of these accounts.

Marital Versus Separate Property

One of the court's most important determinations may be what is separate property and what is a product of the marriage.

Marital property is acquired by either spouse during the marriage and before filing for divorce or executing a separation agreement. This property is subject to equitable division by the judge. Separate property is usually not subject to division and generally includes the following:

- Property acquired before marriage
- Property inherited by one of the spouses
- Property given to one of the spouses only, by someone other than the other spouse
- Property acquired after the final separation
- Increases in the value of separate property

Distinguishing marital from separate property can be difficult. For example, if one spouse owns a home before marriage, this home would ordinarily be considered separate property of the owning spouse. But if the couple lived in the house during the marriage and made improvements to the home, that residence would probably be considered marital property.

Temporary Support Hearings

Either party can file a motion for Pendente Lite Relief (meaning "pending the outcome of litigation"). Under Alabama law, this motion allows one party to ask for a hearing to seek temporary support for paying bills and expenses while the divorce is being finalized. Such support may be essential to you and your family, but there are reasons to avoid a temporary hearing if possible. First, the hearing settles nothing over the long haul. It may be more productive to put your efforts into a final hearing and avoid the expense and time incurred in battling over temporary issues.

The best example of this is a sports analogy. Hardly anyone remembers who wins preseason games in any sport. If we remember anything year to year, it is who won the championship. That's one for the history books and where you want to win.

Also, you lose the element of surprise that can be so effective and satisfying at the trial. You may not want to disclose your secrets, or "hidden ammunition," at a temporary hearing. You may want to surprise the other side with it at trial. Once you reveal a trial issue at a temporary hearing, the other party has an opportunity to dilute the issue before the trial and develop some amazing reason why certain things occurred during the marriage.

You may want to impress the trial judge with your case at a temporary hearing. But you may not gain those points with your judge because he or she may not conduct the temporary hearing. Another attorney appointed as a daily master, or a different judge or court referee, may be on the bench. The main reason to conduct a temporary hearing is to get relief right now. And the rulings in a temporary hearing can drastically impact the final out-come of your case. Consult with your lawyer about the benefits or disadvantages of a temporary hearing.

Sometimes a lawyer will file the necessary pleadings for the temporary hearing but attempt to resolve these matters without a hearing. If settlement is not possible or additional emergencies arise, a hearing is already set.

This temporary hearing can address issues of custody, child support, temporary spousal support, maintenance of insurance, payment of debts, preservation of assets and many other issues. While the steps taken to prepare the case will decide whether you need a temporary hearing, additional judgments must be made about the likelihood of success on these issues.

It is possible to schedule a temporary hearing and find that you have fallen into a trap. One example might be a hearing to determine who should run a family business. The wife, the chief operating officer of the company for many years, may want the husband to leave his job as business manager to reduce conflict and allow her to make the company more successful.

Much to the wife's surprise, the husband may introduce evidence that the wife has been skimming off profits, authorizing shoddy work and drinking on the job. Faced with this situation, the judge might place the husband at the head of the business temporarily and leave the wife out in the cold.

Failing to advise your attorney of potential pitfalls in your case can be a grave mistake. If your attorney is fully advised of possible red flags, he or she can choose the most appropriate course of action to pursue a particular issue. Utilize a temporary relief hearing only when you have exhausted all other remedies.

Learn to accept responsibility for decisions you make after gaining the knowledge to do so. You may not believe you are capable of handling money. But it is usually a lack of experience and confidence, not ability.

CHAPTER 6

Do You Need a Financial Planner?

For most clients, consulting a financial planner during the divorce process can help to meet financial goals. A financial planner can provide useful information about ways to minimize your tax consequences as a result of divorce decisions, help reduce or eliminate budget expenses, develop income options and plan major financial decisions such as retirement or home purchases. You may decide to retain certain assets and sell others. These decisions need to be made with the advice of a financial planner.

Selecting a financial planner is a personal decision, much like selecting a lawyer. Your lawyer should be able to provide you with the names of several reputable financial planners in your community. We have included a list of financial planners in Appendix 2 who have experience in the divorce arena.

The financial advisors at Charles D. Haines, L.L.C., a

Saving Your Assets

Birmingham financial planning firm, offer the following 14 suggestions for establishing financial stability before or after divorce:

1. Establish a hefty emergency fund for contingencies you cannot anticipate. Also, give permission for unusual expenditures. Many divorced people go a little crazy after the settlement with vacations, new cars and homes. Set reasonable limits.

2. Avoid sudden major changes if you can afford to wait. Even when it seems obvious that downsizing is needed, take time to adjust before attempting anything big.

3. Be reluctant to accept illiquid assets or assets with high tax liabilities in any settlement. They can make a settlement that looks like a 50/50 split something much less equal. Even though retirement assets allow a waiver of the 10% penalty for early withdrawal if it is taken in "substantially equal payments over the account holder's life expectancy," it tends to force too much cash out.

4. Begin financial planning prior to a final settlement. Both parties can be greatly helped by seeing how the settlement will affect future plans. Projections should focus on income and expenses, retirement and insurance needs.

5. Factor in long-term care needs when structuring settlement amounts and projecting future cash flows. If you receive a cash settlement, plans for depleting the asset over life to cover living expenses should include holding a reserve for long-term care needs or factoring long-term care insurance premiums into the budget.

6. Parents of special needs children (mentally or physically disabled) need to address lifetime care issues in the settlements. Medicaid eligibility is essential for these children. Usually, it is the only way to get health insurance coverage for them.

7. Life insurance amounts need to cover alimony and child support obligations. To alleviate the high cost to the payor, consider staggering the amounts insurance you carry over time. For example, you might purchase $500,000 coverage for the first 10 years and reduce that amount to $300,000 for the next ten.

8. Pay bills on time, if possible. Repair your credit if needed and build credit if you have none. Checking your credit record is easy and should be done periodically.

9. Both former spouses must work to make up for the financial loss sustained in divorce. Strict budgeting and disciplined savings are needed to get back on track to reaching reasonable retirement and financial security goals. Both should take advantage of all tax-favored savings plans, such as 401(k)s, IRAs and Roth IRAs.

10. Be willing to pay for a good financial planner, attorney and accountant. Bad advice costs so much more in the long run. Check advisors out through their professional associations, other clients and fellow professionals.

11. Determine who is going to pay college costs, including tuition and fees, room and board, sorority/fraternity expenses and educational travel opportunities. Specify a dollar amount or percent.

12. Stock options have value even when the exercise price is higher that the current market price. Have someone do an independent evaluation before determining how to factor options into the settlement.

13. Change your will and beneficiary designations as soon as possible after the divorce. Most people fail to change beneficiaries. For company benefits, there are usually multiple forms to sign; one for the retirement plan(s), group life and accidental death.

14. With the help of a financial planner, learn to make your own financial decisions. Understand that you cannot rely on advisors forever, or substitute them for a former spouse.

This list courtesy of Sherry Robinson, C.P.A., C.F.P.
and Brandy Hydrick, C.F.A., at Charles D. Haines, L.L.C.

Wood ◆ Shaw

"Going through a divorce can be an expensive experience if you don't receive proper accounting advice. The rules are very complex with respect to alimony and property settlements and tax advice will help you achieve fair and expected results."

Anthony J. DiPiazza, Birmingham Accountant

CHAPTER 7

Other Professionals Can Help

A divorce can involve the drafting of several documents in a lawyer's office and that can be handled in a matter of hours. Or it can consume months of negotiations and settlement discussions to resolve the intricacies of your particular case. For more complicated cases, you may need professional help planning and making decisions. The professionals who can prove most helpful to you include lawyers in specialties other than family law, accountants, financial planners, estate planners, psychologists, therapists and clergy. Appendices 1-7 are lists of these professionals with experience helping divorcing people.

Lawyers in Other Practice Areas

Your lawyer may wish to retain additional legal counsel to help assist with other matters related to your case. You may need a criminal lawyer to handle harassment or assault matters related to the divorce. You may require business counsel or tax lawyers to help with certain issues related to the case, such as the division of a business or tax consequences. You may need a lawyer familiar with certain corporate documents to determine their validity or advise the best means of attacking the documents or the dissolution of a company. Your lawyer's firm may handle all these matters in-house.

In this era of legal specialists, attorneys who concentrate in family law must have a wide range of legal knowledge. It can be difficult to be an expert in taxes or criminal law as well as a top matrimonial lawyer at the same time. We frequently team with outside counsel so that we can concentrate on the entire case and obtain specific advice on certain matters in our client's interest. Large, complicated cases involving complex property arrangements often demand a team approach. Address the use of outside counsel as a resource with your lawyer and make certain he or she is comfortable with the use of other lawyers who can help if the need arises.

Accountants

Increasingly, accountants and bookkeepers are needed during a divorce action to determine when tax returns should be filed and whether they are accurate. Certified public accountants may be used to audit or value a business. The accountant may also estimate the tax consequences associated with various options available during the settlement of the divorce. You may already have an accountant to help make some of these decisions. Or you may want to get independent advice to make certain your spouse's financial actions have been appropriate. Your lawyer should be able to advise you about the need for an accountant in your case as well as recommend certain accountants (preferably certified public accountants) to help you in this regard. Appendix 1 contains a list of accountants throughout the state with experience handling divorce-related matters.

Accountants can audit and calculate the personal expenditures related to a budget. An accountant can often take your personal home and family financial records and create a spreadsheet to show your family's average spending per category over the past several years. Many times this is necessary when a spouse claims to make considerably less income than the family has been spending. An audit often demonstrates a budget several times higher than the actual income being claimed. Thus, the question at trial becomes "how have you been able to live on X if you only make Y?" Does this person have another source of income he or she is not reporting? Only a detailed analysis of income and expenses can determine what is actually going on.

One of the most effective ways an accountant can be used is to evaluate and audit business financial records. The tax returns of privately owned businesses are often vague and uninformative, especially to the untrained eye.

The actual bank and other financial records generally prove more clearly the actual spending and income of the business. As with most financial dealings related to divorce, this can work both ways. Many times this type of audit will show that a spouse is receiving benefits and other perks from the company far beyond the reported income. These expenditures may be included as income for the spouse and lead to alterations in child support and alimony payments. Conversely, if you are the payor spouse and you are involved in the business, you need to be thoroughly prepared to prove your actual income.

Often family owned businesses pay some personal expenses for family members who work in the business. If you are paid out of the business and those amounts aren't reported as personal income, be prepared to substantiate that these amounts should not figure into child support and alimony calculations. Many spouses use the business account to pay for such personal expenditures as house payments, personal automobile expenses and luxury travel expenditures. Simply because these amounts are deducted as business expenses does not mean they are legitimate.

Many times the accountant simply reports the information provided to him. A close examination of company records must be made to determine if the business has the resources to pay personal expenses.

John West, a partner in the accounting firm of Donaldson, Holman & West, says owner/employees of closely held businesses typically rely on the business for most of their income. "Closely held businesses often have no excess cash available and depend upon cash flow from ongoing operations to provide the owner with income and benefits," he said. "The business can be very valuable but have no excess cash or liquid assets available. Also, the value and control of a family business can be a very emotional issue. Structured settlements should allow closely held business to survive and flourish so the family can maximize the value from the business's continuing cash flows to the benefit of all the parties."

Estate Planners

Many clients fail to address their estate planning concerns both during the divorce and afterward. The typical married couple has a will that states if one spouse dies, all assets go to the surviving spouse. If you are concerned about the terms of your will, consult your lawyer once the divorce is filed. Understand that the terms and conditions of your new will may be used against you in your divorce proceeding. If you eliminate your spouse entirely from your will during the pendency of the case, the trial court may view this action as punitive.

Often clients fail to update their estate documents even after the divorce. Many times, the parties do not have a will or the will is so outdated that it does not adequately address a change in circumstances. You may not recognize the tax consequences associated with the assets you receive under the settlement agreement and fail to make adequate estate planning preparations. An estate planner can advise you and your divorce lawyer about tax consequences associated with certain actions or positions in the case.

Estate planner C. Fred Daniels, an attorney with the firm of Cabaniss, Johnston, Gardner, Dumas & O'Neal, says one of the most common estate planning problems he sees after a divorce is the failure to make changes in beneficiary designations. "A divorce decree cannot change the beneficiary designations of employer group-term life insurance, 401(k) plans, profit sharing plans or pension plans," he explains. "The paperwork to make these changes must be completed on the employer's forms and submitted to the employer in order to remove a former spouse as the beneficiary of the plan. Similarly, beneficiary designations must be changed for individual retirement accounts and life insurance policies by amending the forms. The most commonly litigated questions at death following a divorce are caused by the failure to complete these changes in beneficiary forms."

Tax attorney Bill Bryant says the transfer of assets between spouses in a divorce is generally tax-free. "But the division of certain assets such as family business interests and retirement benefits, the structuring of post-divorce payments and the utilization of insurance and trusts present traps for the unwary," says Bryant. "By the same token, there are planning opportunities to minimize estate and income taxes and control the management and ultimate disposition of one's assets, including assets that must be allocated to the support of divorce obligations."

See Appendix 3 for a list of estate planners around the state who deal with divorce problems.

Psychologists/Psychiatrists/Therapists

Anger and confusion is normally associated with non-financial matters in a divorce. The stress of adjusting financially to a new lifestyle can cause its own problems. Counseling with a psychologist, psychiatrist or therapist is the perfect antidote for this stress. People make foolish or irresponsible decisions due to the emotional pressure of a divorce. Keep yourself in the best state of mind possible during the time you are making these life-changing decisions. Seek the help of a counselor to deal with the issues related to the divorce or the problems associated with actions that have occurred during the marriage.

This advice comes with a caveat if the custody of minor children is at stake. In such cases, the other side may obtain the records of psychologists or psychiatrists during the litigation. A judge can override the time-honored rule that counseling records are privileged and not discoverable if the welfare of children is at stake. The private things you tell a counselor can come out at trial. Seek the advice of your lawyer immediately if you are seeing a counselor or have seen one in the past.

How you deal with questions of adultery, substance abuse, domestic violence and other issues on the dark side of family life are important even when only finances are at issue, since the court uses fault as a factor in deciding the division of property.

Counselors can help, but this may not be the best time to make an honest attempt to change. During a divorce your every action is placed under a microscope and examined for everyone to see and judge.

There are different options available relating to counseling. Each generally depends upon your specific situation. Psychiatrists and psychologists are available, as well as licensed therapists. Professionals generally have a primary concentration. One psychologist may see adults primarily, whereas another may see children. Other professionals may deal only with marriage counseling and refuse to become involved in divorce cases that result in litigation.

Dr. Karen Turnbow, a psychologist with Alabama Psychotherapy & Wellness Center, deals primarily with children in her practice. Even on the financial side of divorce, she sees parents putting their children in the middle. "One of the most damaging things I have observed is parents using their children as messengers so they do not have to interact with one another," she says.

Saving Your Assets

"Many times parents ask their children about child support checks, money for extra activities or visitation issues. This, of course, places children in the middle of ongoing animosities. If children carry the message, they often have to deal with an angry reaction from the other parent. If they choose not to carry the message, they are often made to feel guilty or disloyal. Parents must put their differences aside and communicate directly with one another. Many times I ask parents to show that their love for the children exceeds their anger toward their ex-spouse."

Sometimes parents use children to pick a fight with the ex over money. The parents wind up screaming at each other over the cost of a toy or tuition to a camp. They give children the impression that without this issue, the parents would agree. Children feel they are responsible for parental blowups.

While being friends with your children is a good thing, many divorced people take it too far. Making children confidantes or best friends is not healthy. Counselor Nancy Wasson says she sees children who are used as confidants by one or both parents.

"Children are told all the reasons why one parent thinks the other parent is inadequate or horrible," she says. "Children need to be protected from a rehashing of the many hurtful things that contributed to the divorce. It is not fair to smash the idealized picture of the other parent just because one parent wants to vent and thinks the children should know the 'truth.' There is not one truth, just varying perceptions and viewpoints based on experience. Children find out for themselves as time goes by whether the other parent is dependable, loving, honest or trustworthy."

See Appendix 4 for a list of psychologists, psychiatrists, counselors and therapists across the state.

"Some parents are unwilling to accept the court's ruling on a money issue and they frequently ask the children about it. This places children in a difficult position concerning decisions they cannot legally make."

Dr. Karen Turnbow

Church Counselors

Another valuable source of assistance during a divorce can be found in your church, synagogue or other spiritual support group. Many churches all across the state have specific divorce recovery programs that provide valuable assistance. Several of these programs are listed in Appendix 5. Your pastor, minister, rabbi or other religious leader may provide valuable counseling during this process. Many times this assistance is free and can provide a valuable outreach for you during this trying time. Often these groups bring in experts such as attorneys, financial planners, accountants and counselors who convey worthwhile information at no cost.

Even if you are not associated with a church, most churches will gladly welcome the opportunity to provide assistance during this time. Many times these programs involve people who have already experienced a divorce helping you deal with the process of the ongoing divorce or its aftermath.

Wood ◆ Shaw

10 Effective Ways to Save Money On Your Divorce

Almost no one is happy with the results after telling your lawyer to win at all costs. Below are 10 very general tips on getting the most for your divorce dollar.

1. Collect as much financial and personal information as possible on your own before seeing an attorney.
2. Don't act impulsively, such as leaving the marital residence or abandoning your children. If both of you can stay in the home, you can save a bundle.
3. If you suspect your spouse is hiding assets, help your attorney find them.
4. If you are doing anything to contribute to the divorce, such as having an affair, drinking too much or gambling, stop it now.
5. Try not to argue incessantly with your estranged spouse. Heated talk leads to retaliation that costs money in professional fees.
6. Be cost effective in fighting for personal property.
7. Consider tax consequences when dividing property.
8. Sweat the details. For instance, if your spouse agrees to keep health insurance on the children, check with the insurance company to make sure it's in force.
9. If you can work out custody of your children, do so. A full-blown custody fight is very expensive.
10. Make sure life insurance is in place to cover alimony or child support payments over time, in case the payor spouse dies.

CHAPTER 8

Professional Fees

How Much Will This Case Cost?

Fees paid to your attorney and other professionals are usually the largest expenses in the divorce. The settlement agreement should address payment of attorney's fees. Payment of fees to accountants and business experts who trace assets or research business values are often part of the legal bill.

Typically, a settlement agreement will either state that each party pay their own fees or that one party shall pay all or part of the other party's fees up to a specified amount. The agreement may say the fees shall be equally divided between the parties. In a contested divorce, the award of attorney's fees by the court is discretionary and is based upon the facts of the case and the overall terms of the property settlement.

Keeping Fees Down

Each time you meet with your lawyer, the staff works on your case or you speak on the telephone, additional time and money is used up.

Don't confuse the billing policies of divorce lawyers with advertisements you see on television for accident cases where the lawyer promises "no fee unless we collect." Alabama State Bar rules prohibit a lawyer from charging a contingency fee (a percentage of the recovery) in a divorce. Some clients look at attorney's fees on a contingency basis, even though there is no such agreement. These clients feel they don't have to actually pay the fees unless they get a windfall at the courthouse. No one really enjoys paying the lawyer for a divorce, but avoiding payment is not the way to keep fees down. Payment in advance was designed for this type of client.

Let your attorney know that money is an issue. Because your attorney usually works by the hour, don't use him or her as a sounding board for all the "he said, she said" gripes that are common in a contested divorce. Gossiping will cost you money. It makes more sense to write down what you want your attorney to know and the questions you need answered. Take these lists to your next appointment.

If you call your lawyer at home or on weekends, just to vent complaints, you will pay more for your divorce. Instead, talk to the secretary or legal assistant when possible. Let your attorney know you are doing that intentionally, so as not to waste his time...and your money. If there is an emergency, though, it may be necessary to call your attorney at home. It should be a matter of great urgency that cannot wait until morning. You and your attorney should agree about what specifically constitutes an emergency.

Unfortunately, you cannot control actions by the other side. How combative the opposing party gets can affect the cost of your case. If your spouse demands his or her day in court or will not bend on the simplest property issues, you may be in for an expensive battle.

Who Pays Legal Fees?

It's not true that the party filing the divorce is responsible for attorney's fees. In most cases, each spouse pays his or her legal bills. If the fees are not awarded to your spouse, or if he or she fails to pay them, you are responsible for them. Most divorce experts require you to pay fees incurred before the case is resolved. Then if the other side is ordered to pay, the lawyer reimburses you. In most cases, divorce experts will not take on a litigated divorce hoping the other side will pay the fees.

Taking the case on that basis would mean the lawyer doesn't get paid for a long time or you are left with a huge bill you hope your spouse has to pay. If your lawyer has done a good job representing you, your spouse will not be thrilled to pay the attorney's fees of the person who was so effective.

If there is a large amount of marital property, think of legal fees as an investment. Consider the enormous amount of money at stake in many divorces, including the cumulative value of child support and alimony and the related property settlement issues. For example, a 35-year-old woman who requests $1,500 per month in periodic alimony could easily receive more than half a million dollars over her lifetime. It's a sum the husband in that case doesn't want to consider. Coupled with child support awards, property settlements, equity in the home, retirement plans, insurance considerations, debts, and college expenses, the value of an estate can range from several hundred thousand dollars to several million dollars in a divorce of middle class people. With that much money on the line, hiring a skilled matrimonial law specialist is a prudent use of your funds.

Ask For a Statement

Review regular statements from your attorney to track the time spent on your case and the balance of your retainer. Legal time can add up quickly and surpass the value of the assets in question. Even when this happens, you are obligated to pay the fees.

Preparing a case for trial requires many hours of your lawyer's time. Some clients say they want their lawyer to do whatever it takes. Some lawyers make the mistake of telling you the balance due at the end of the divorce. But you may end up owing far more than you expected, so make sure to request billing statements if your attorney does not provide them.

Most attorneys bill separately for expenses incurred in the case, including the following:

Filing fees – These costs are incurred by the attorney in the course of representation, and are generally due at the time the services are rendered. The average filing fee for a divorce action in Alabama is approximately $154.

Deposition costs – They depend on the length and complexity of the deposition. The lawyer pays a court reporter to record the testimony in the deposition. A typical divorce deposition will cost anywhere from $300 to $500 or more for the court reporter. This does not include the attorney's time associated with preparing for and taking the deposition.

Process server fees – These are charges for serving the opposing party with pleadings, subpoenas and other related documents. If time is important, a special process server can serve the documents immediately, while the local sheriff's department sometimes takes several weeks to accomplish the same thing. The fee for service of documents by a process server generally runs from $50 to $100 or more, depending on how difficult it is to locate and serve the individual.

Copies and faxes – You may be charged for these as well as other costs associated with preparing the case. It is always wise to familiarize yourself with the anticipated costs to avoid confusion.

Litigation Budget

Although your lawyer cannot say exactly how much your divorce will cost, it stands to reason that a case which takes more than a year to resolve will cost much more than one that is settled in a few days. The following litigation budget (Figure 1) may help you comprehend the vast number of issues and large amounts of time that may be required to resolve your case. This list is merely a guide to the potential cost of your case. Many of the listed items may not be necessary in your case and many other items not listed may be required.

Potential Litigation Budget
Figure 1

TASK	PROJECTED TIME LIKELY TO BE INCURRED
Meetings with Client	
Drafting Initial Pleadings in the Case	
Drafting Temporary Support Documents	
Drafting Temporary Restraining Orders	
Drafting Protection from Abuse Pleadings	
Drafting Discovery Including Interrogatories, Request for Production, Request for Admissions and Notices of Deposition	
Meetings with Client During the Pendency of the Case	
Telephone Conferences with Client During the Pendency of the Case	
Meeting with Witnesses	
Preparing for Hearings	
Preparing Client for Hearings	
Preparing for Depositions	
Preparing Client for Depositions	
Reviewing Pleadings from Opposing Party and Responding to Same	
Taking Depositions of Opposing Party	
Attending Deposition of Client	
Taking Depositions of Expert Witnesses and Preparing for Same	
Taking Depositions of Other Witnesses and Preparing for Same	
Attending Temporary Support Hearing	
Attending the Trial	
Court Reporter's Expenses	
Photocopy Expenses	
Postage Expenses	
Deposition Expenses	

Private Investigator Expenses	
Long Distance Charges	
Travel Expenses	
Costs	
Reviewing Financial Records	
Reviewing Corporate Financial Records	
Meeting with Accountant Concerning Audit of Records	
Expert Witness Cost	
Costs	
Reviewing Medical Record Issues	
Preparing Subpoena's for Witnesses and Documents	
Reviewing Information Received Pursuant to Subpoena's	
Reviewing Client's Financial Information	
Reviewing Opposing Parties Financial Information	
Preparing Responses to Interrogatories and Request for Production	
Reviewing Opposing Parties Responses to Interrogatories and Request for Production	
Preparing for and Attending Trial Settings	
Preparing for the Trial	
Preparing for the next Day's Trial in the Evening	
Miscellaneous Items	
Unanticipated Issues	
Subtotal Expenses	
Subtotal Paralegal Time	
Subtotal Attorney Time	
Total	

The goal of providing these listed items in the litigation budget is to help you realize the large number of activities that may be required in your divorce. If your lawyer bills $200 or more per hour, you can run up a significant bill just meeting with him or her. Add in the legal and paralegal work that must be performed as a result of those meetings and you may be looking at significant costs.

At the same time, flat fee pricing may affect the quality of legal services you receive. If a lawyer quotes you an incredibly low flat fee, question whether that lawyer will dedicate the time necessary to perform many of the tasks listed above. Generally, our firm will not represent individuals in a litigated divorce case on a flat fee basis. We may charge a flat fee if the parties reach a settlement, and even then we limit the hours we will devote. Otherwise, you would be charged a flat fee for a case that is resolved fairly quickly or the law firm could end up handling a case involving many more hours than what was budgeted.

Wood ◆ Shaw

Legal Fees An Investment

Client Tammi Manley says the money she spent hiring an expert in family law was worth it. "I realized how important being an active partner in a business and marriage really was when my marriage ended," she says. "I was aware of our financial status and able to gather all information needed to defend my place in the business. I asked my attorney to make the best objective decisions for me. The legal fees involved in hiring an expert in my case were far outweighed by the additional assets I was awarded."

PART TWO

Settlement:
Dividing Assets, Absorbing Debt

"The smartest thing
I did during my
marriage was manage
my money. When my
husband left me, I had
a complete financial
picture. I knew what I
had to fight for . . . and
what I stood to lose."

Sharon, divorced mother of one daughter

CHAPTER 9

Understanding Your Budget

O
ne of the most important steps to a successful financial divorce is to determine what income is available to meet an anticipated budget. Once you set your budget, it takes a simple mathematical analysis to look at the level and sources of income and determine whether they are adequate to cover your expenditures.

Lisa Woods, a matrimonial lawyer, says that especially in long-term marriages, the parties often settle into a habit of not sharing financial information. One spouse pays the bills while the other person just trusts that it's being done correctly. "It is difficult to get a working knowledge of the parties' assets and liabilities after the marriage has broken down," says Woods. "The wiser course would be for both spouses to have a working understanding of finances throughout the course of the marriage."

Saving Your Assets

The first step is to determine what your anticipated expenses might be after divorce. The budget chart on the next page (Figure 2) can help calculate your expenses. This chart also helps identify areas in which you have little or no documentation. Your lawyer will need documentation of each of the listed expenses to prove these items at trial. This proof is generally found in cancelled checks, receipts and credit card statements. Document how you came up with the numbers listed on your proposed budget without simply guessing.

Anyone who prepares a budget probably begins with an optimistic wish list. Fill out this chart based on your actual spending, not your desired level of spending. Make sure you account for all your typical spending, not just the big items. You may be surprised how much cash you dispense through discretionary spending each month, using ATM withdrawals.

Once you determine these expenses, compare them to your available income. That should tell you how well you can maintain your current lifestyle after the divorce. For example, assume the expenses of each spouse total $5,000 per month. If the personal income of the recipient spouse is approximately $1,500 per month and the estimated child support received is approximately $1,000 per month, that person is $2,500 short of the proposed budget. Alimony may or may not cover the shortfall, depending on the resources available in your household. For the payor spouse, providing $1,000 in child support and $1,500 in alimony may leave you with less available income than you budgeted. Revisit your budget to determine whether there should be significant changes. Most people fail to go through this exercise before getting a divorce because they do not want to know they will not

Sample Budget Chart
Figure 2

WOOD & SHAW, LLC, ATTORNEYS AT LAW

EXPENSES	MONTHLY PAYMENT
FIXED EXPENSES	$
House payment	$
Insurance	$
Home	$
Automobile	$
Health	$
Life	$
Other	$
Taxes - Home	$
FLEXIBLE EXPENSES	$
Electricity	$
Gas or Oil (Heat)	$
Telephone	$
Water and Sewer	$
Cable Television	$
Pest Control	$
Yard Care	$
Household Help	$
Repair/Maintenance	$
Other	$
FOOD	$
Groceries	$
Restaurants	$
Lunches	$
TRANSPORTATION	$
Car payment	$
Gas and Oil	$
Repairs/Maintenance	$
Auto Tag and Taxes	$
CHILDREN	$
Private School, Tutors, etc.	$
Activities (Sports, Music, Scouts, etc)	$
School lunches	$
Other school costs	$
CLOTHING/PERSONAL	$
Clothes - You	$
Clothes - Children	$
Shoes	$
Accessories	$
Laundry/Dry Cleaning	$
Beauty Shop/Barber	$
Cosmetics	$
ENTERTAINMENT	$
Newspapers	$
Magazines, Books	$
Sports, Movies, etc.	$
Vacations	$
Other Entertainment	$
EDUCATION	$
Tuition	$
Textbooks, Notebooks, Binders, etc.	$
MISCELLANEOUS COSTS/EXPENSES	$
Religious Contribution	$
Gifts (Birthdays, Holidays, etc.)	$
Taxes Withheld	$

Savings	$
IRA, Other Retirement	$
MEDICAL	$
Doctors	$
Dentists	$
Orthodontist	$
Optometrist	$
Medicine/Prescriptions	$
Other	$
CREDIT CARDS (Itemize with Balance Due)	Minimum Payment
	$
	$
	$
	$
	$
	$
	$
	$
PERSONAL LOANS (Itemize)	$
	$
OTHER	$
	$
TOTAL EXPENSES	$
TOTAL PERSONAL NET INCOME	$
ALIMONY PAYMENTS	$
CHILD SUPPORT PAYMENTS	$
SURPLUS OR DEFICIT	$

have enough money. Many budgets that seem workable at first glance fail to consider the tax ramifications inherent in the analysis, making the financial house of cards doomed from the very beginning.

Paying for the House During the Divorce

The major expense during most divorces is the family home, and it's also the primary source of friction. One spouse or the other usually wants to stay in the house. Whether you can pay for it and another residence for the other party is another question. It is important to factor in all the housing expenses – the mortgage payment, taxes, insurance, yard care, repair and upkeep.

If you want to keep the house, look at the possibility of refinancing the mortgage to achieve a lower monthly payment. This may give you enough cash to pay bills in the short term. By refinancing, you may be able to release your spouse from the mortgage obligation in exchange for allowing you to keep the house. This is often attractive because even though the court awards one party the house, the mortgage company does not have to release the other party from the mortgage indebtedness.

"When purchasing or refinancing a home, the loan with the lowest interest or the larger down payment isn't always the best loan," says Randy Brown, vice president of New South Federal Savings Bank. "Often a higher rate — which might be tax deductible — can more than offset mortgage insurance premiums associated with a traditional conforming loan. A smaller down payment can free up money needed for other expenses. Refinancing can allow you to consolidate high interest rate bank cards and department store cards."

It may be more affordable for you to sell the residence and purchase a newer home that requires fewer repairs. Your lawyer can put you in touch with a professional realtor who can help you with your housing options, as well as a mortgage lender to help you refinance your current home or purchase another.

Appendix 6 contains a list of several mortgage companies in Alabama.

Regulating Your Work Schedule

Many spouses who stayed home during the marriage or worked part-time may intend to continue this same role after the divorce. Some spouses who worked overtime or more than one job during the marriage might be experiencing burnout and hope to reduce his or her workload to a regular 40-hour week. Will your income options meet your current budget expenses? Perhaps you can cut some of your expenses, so that you can get by with less income. If it is difficult to cut expenses, you may need to increase your income. This may mean going back to work or adding to your workload. The same goes for spouses who opt for flexible work schedules, such as four-day work weeks, part-time work or flex time.

Analyze every option and recognize each option's impact on the overall financial package. For example, day care costs may need to be considered in determining your child support expenses.

Many times, a spouse needs the health insurance benefits provided by a full-time employer. It is often less expensive to maintain a job providing excellent benefits than to pay the tremendously high premiums often charged for individual health insurance coverage.

Alimony can factor into your decision to go back to work. Parties who expect alimony (usually the wife) may have been in a marriage that lasted only a short time. Your lawyer may advise you that under the circumstances, alimony is unlikely to be awarded. So you need to look at other employment options. It doesn't matter if your former spouse promised you would never have to work again. The question becomes whether the court will require a significant alimony award. If the answer is probably no, then you need to look at your options for cutting expenses and gaining a greater source of income.

Forced Savings for Emergencies

One client recommends developing an emergency savings plan during this critical period. She relates how she decided to take a job that paid only commission. Her ex-husband did not pay regular child support for their two children, but she had confidence in her ability to earn an income and did not want to be obligated to a job limited to a salary. She also wanted to save for her children's future. Not knowing what her income would be, she looked at some "forced savings plans," decided what amount she wanted to save every month and obligated herself to these plans.

She remembers receiving the annual statement on these plans and realizing she had not missed the money. She survived the year financially and saved some for her children. The discipline of forced savings enabled her to show something for her hard work.

If the mortgage is a joint debt, both parties remain liable even if one transfers interest to the other. In most cases, you can only remove a party's name from the mortgage by paying off the debt or refinancing it.

CHAPTER 10

Asset #1:
Who Gets the House?

The question after divorce usually is not who gets the house but who can afford it. Many times people fight over the house only to find that neither can afford it alone. It is often difficult to make the house payment while paying child support and alimony payments, as well as provide for two separate households. Whether you want to keep the house becomes irrelevant without the ability to pay for it.

An experienced matrimonial lawyer will examine your financial ability to maintain the residence before recommending how it should be handled after the divorce. This also involves a careful review of your income and debts and the effect of child support or alimony payments. The budget included in Appendix 12 will help determine whether you can afford to keep the residence. Realizing you cannot afford the house may shock you, but it is better to learn this early in the process. You don't want to spend a year fighting for an asset you cannot keep.

Does Your Spouse Have to Move Out When You File?

The mere filing of a divorce does not mean either spouse has to move out of the house immediately. Except in cases where severe violence has been proven, the court may leave both parties in the house and maintain the status quo of the marriage until the final resolution of the case. While this may sound like institutional insanity, it is often the result of limited financial options. If only one party has an income, funds may not be available to pay for separate housing.

The party who is paying for the house may not want the divorce and may not want to move out. There is also method to this madness. Parties who remain in the same house are often motivated to settle the divorce so they can restart their lives elsewhere. If they live separately and one party is paying the mortgage, it may take forever to bring the spouse who is comfortably living in the house to consider settlement options.

Common sense tells you people going through a divorce do not get along very well and do not want to be around each other. If custody, visitation and financial issues can be resolved, it is often better for the parties to live separately during the process. All of these issues need to be addressed with your lawyer and made a part of your initial considerations and overall strategy before filing for divorce.

If a temporary hearing is required to determine who gets possession of the home during the divorce, the court will consider compelling reasons why one spouse should be removed, such as violence or heated arguments. If these arguments occur in front of the children, it may be more appropriate to separate the parties. The court usually allows the party receiving custody to keep the children in familiar surroundings during a chaotic time in everyone's lives. If both parties realize the house must be sold, it could be placed on the market. If the house sells, the equity proceeds can be held in trust pending a resolution of the case.

Gaining custody of your children is generally easier to accomplish if you and the children are still living in the marital residence. The court wants to keep the children's lives as uninterrupted as possible. It is helpful to show the children in their own bedrooms, with their own toys and friends nearby.

As a rule, the party receiving temporary custody of the children maintains temporary possession of the home because it is the children's residence.

Clients sometimes leave the home due to fear of violence but leave the children in the home with the "violent" person. If you are so fearful of violence that you flee the home, why leave the children there? If these issues are present in your case, get sound legal advice before proceeding with any course of action. If the safety of you and your children is threatened, seek the assistance of the police and leave your home until your safety can be ensured. In such a case, seek immediate legal counsel so you can get the assistance of the court.

Final Options for Handling the Residence

Once you decide whether to keep the marital residence, several options are available that can be addressed in a settlement agreement, including:

- Selling the home and dividing the equity
- Transferring the home from one spouse to another
- Transferring the home to one spouse for a set time and then selling it and dividing the equity
- Deeding the home to one spouse in exchange for a cash payment of the equity

Selling the Home and Dividing the Equity

The most clean-cut option is to place the residence on the market immediately, sell it and divide the proceeds. Sometimes, one party receives all the equity. Or the parties divide it in some pro-rata fashion. The property should be appraised and listed for the appraisal amount or for an amount suggested by a realtor. You may not have to incur appraisal costs if the realtor knows local market values. If you pretty well know the value of the property, you can use the realtor's opinion. An appraisal is needed when there are few properties comparable to your home now on the market. Appraisers are licensed and bonded. If you need an appraisal, their opinions are more authoritative if they have to testify in court about the value of your home.

When the parties cannot agree on the value of the residence, each party may want to conduct an independent appraisal of the property. If the two appraisals differ greatly, the parties can select a third appraiser who will value the residence. It is less expensive to have this appraiser evaluate the two appraisals rather than value the property. This procedure can be costly and can be resolved much easier by naming a realtor in the agreement and stating that the parties will follow his or her advice. It is common for the parties to differ on what repairs are needed to place the residence on the market. The realtor can often resolve these issues more objectively and wisely than two people who don't respect each other's opinion. If the realtor suggests certain improvements to the residence, he or she can arrange for the work without incurring a great deal of extra cost. The settlement agreement should state who pays the mortgage, taxes, insurance and utilities during the time the residence is on the market. The agreement should require the person who lives in the house to keep the house in a clean and orderly fashion while it is on the market. The agreement should specify who will provide routine maintenance and upkeep, as well as who pays the cost of reasonable and necessary repairs such as heating, cooling, roofing and structural repairs.

When the parties do not have funds for necessary repairs or improvements, one party can borrow money for the repairs. The proceeds of the sale can pay off the loan, with the remainder divided between the parties.

An agreement should specify that when the house is sold, the following items will be deducted from the gross sales price (if applicable):

- Mortgage payoff
- Brokerage commission
- Legal fees related to the sale
- Repairs or improvements
- Costs of sale
- Payment of other debts specified in the settlement agreement
- Equity each party will receive

Judicial Sale

As a safeguard, you may want to include a judicial sale provision in your agreement. If the house is not sold within a certain time, usually six months, under this provision the court can order the house sold at auction and any remaining proceeds divided.

This should only be employed as a last ditch
court ordered sale never realizes the maximum ι
little equity in the house and one party bears the
this may be the only option available to get out fɪ   ᴖι that
mortgage obligation. If one party continuously inhibits the sale,
such as not providing maintenance and upkeep or not keeping the
residence clean when it is being shown, the threat of a judicial sale
may provide the necessary incentive to prevent this behavior.
Unless specified, anyone, including the parties, can bid on the
house at a judicial sale. Often you can purchase your own property at the judicial sale at a greatly discounted price and end up
with a valuable asset.

Transferring the Home
from One Spouse to Another

Your settlement agreement can specify that one party transfer his or her interest in the residence to the other party. Usually
the party giving up the house gets some other consideration, such
as a larger share of retirement accounts, personal property or a
family business. It is important that both parties be aware of what
they are getting or giving away under this scenario. Specific language concerning the valuation of the residence may be required.

Many parties feel they can receive more value from the residence under this scenario, especially if the other party values the
residence so much that he or she is willing to overpay other assets
for it. The residence may not be worth as much as one party
thinks, and if you sold it the house might stay on the market for a
long time. The agreement should also specify that the parties exe-

cute the necessary warranty or quitclaim deeds to transfer their interest and specify responsibility for the mortgage indebtedness as well as taxes and other expenses.

If the party responsible for paying the mortgage defaults, the mortgage company may look to the other spouse for payment of the debt, even though there is no longer any vested interest. The mortgage obligation remains on both parties' credit reports and has to be addressed in future loan applications. Many times this can be handled by showing a creditor a copy of the divorce decree indicating the spouse who is responsible for the mortgage obligation. If you are concerned that your soon-to-be ex may not pay the mortgage obligation, address what happens to the property in that event.

The settlement agreement can specify that if the responsible party becomes delinquent on the mortgage obligation, the residence can be sold. It becomes a balancing act of determining the value for one party to stay in the residence while leaving the mortgage in place, versus selling the residence to clear up that obligation.

Compare the amount of the mortgage payment on the residence to a monthly apartment rental. You may find your mortgage payment is less than the going rate for an apartment of similar size in your area of choice. In this case, remain in the residence and retain the stability of that choice.

This is a large part of the original analysis that must be made concerning whether the parties should attempt to keep the home. You may believe that you can't afford to keep your marital residence, but the other housing options in the area may be even more expensive.

Transferring the Home to One Spouse For a Certain Number of Years and then Selling it

Another settlement option is for one party to have sole use of the home for a specified period of time, then selling it and dividing the equity. Many parties utilize this option when there are young children and an immediate sale of the home would disrupt their lives. The agreement may award the residence to the custodial parent until the children turn age 19, complete college or until that parent remarries. This arrangement provides the stability of the original home during a difficult adjustment period. Requiring children to pack up and move to a new residence can be extremely disruptive. It may be wiser to allow the children to remain in the residence until a later date.

Both parties may want the parent with primary custody of the children to stay in the home because it is close to the children's schools. Consider the school district you want on the front end. Many times, parties will agree to divide the equity after the children have completed a particular grade. The settlement agreement should specify how long the spouse has use of the residence and what events trigger a sale. The agreement should state who is to make the mortgage payment during this period and who is to provide routine maintenance and upkeep as well as reasonable and necessary repairs such as structural, heating and cooling.

If the equity is to be divided at a later date, the agreement should specify whether the equity is set at the time of the divorce or the time of sale. If you have made all the payments since the divorce, you may not want to share the appreciation in the residence with your former spouse. If the parties specify an amount to be paid at the time of sale, decide what happens if the net equity is not sufficient to make the payment. If the agreement is not specific, one party may be required to pay the other more than the net equity at the time of sale. This situation can be avoided if adequate planning is given to the language and value specified in the agreement.

Deeding the Home to One Spouse For a Cash Equity Payment

Another option is for one party to pay the other a specified sum for the marital residence at the time of settlement. If there is adequate money available to make such a payment, this can bring finality to the house issue and the overall divorce as well and could be less complicated than a transfer at some future date.   The terms of payment must be addressed in the settlement agreement, along with the designation for payment of the mortgage obligation. In addition, the issues discussed earlier concerning the existing mortgage indebtedness must also be addressed. Unless the house is refinanced, both parties remain obligated on the existing mortgage.

Tax Consequences from the Sale of the Home

Tax consequences associated with the transfer or sale of the residence to a third party could affect the value of the award. Conversely, there may be no tax consequences if the property is transferred from one spouse to the other as part of the divorce decree. Contact a tax professional to make certain you are aware of the taxes. You may, for example, be responsible for capital gains taxes associated with the appreciation over the original purchase price. Usually, you must adhere to specific time limits for transferring the equity into a new residence to avoid additional taxes. This is a frequently changing area in the tax code. Make certain you know the current law.

There may be more tax advantages to using equity in the home for the payment of certain debts than to cash in a retirement plan or other more heavily taxed account such as one containing stocks and bonds. The intricacies involved in the taxes and transfer of accounts and property need to be considered in their totality rather than as individual decisions.

What a Judge May Do With the Home

In a divorce that goes to trial, the court may consider any of the options discussed as well as looking at other creative alternatives. Most often, the judge will order the home sold immediately and the equity divided or awarded to one party. If the judge does not order a sale, he or she may award the home to one party and specify who is responsible for the mortgage payment. Or he may specify that one party receive the house for a certain number of years and then the house will be sold with the equity divided.

Under this last option, the trial court rarely caps the equity at its current rate. No one can predict how much the house will be worth years from now. The equity is usually divided when it is sold.

If one party has significant emotional ties to the residence, the settlement agreement should address how the house will be handled rather than risking a court-ordered sale. On the other hand, if the parties have spent many hours negotiating the value of the residence, it may be easier to let a judge handle the division of property. Many judges say it is easier to divide a stack of money than a house or a business. If the value is disputed, the court often orders the house sold and any proceeds split between the parties.

Buying a Home After the Divorce

Review the housing options available to you after the divorce. Many people looking at real estate suffer from sticker shock and must adjust to current market prices. Decide what type of house you can afford and address the following areas in looking at a new residence:

- How much will the home cost?
- Will it be in the same school district?
- How much down payment will be required?
- What type of mortgage is available?

Mortgage broker Rob Coats says you should ask yourself if the home is the best use of your available cash (down payment) and monthly expense. "Your initial meeting with a mortgage professional will give you answers regarding down payment, maximum payment that you can qualify for and the obstacles you will encounter during the process," Coats says. "You will receive better opinions about what you may accomplish if you know what is possible from the settlement. The more information the mortgage professional is given, the better his advice."

Randy Brown, vice president of New South Federal Savings Bank, says a home usually is your largest single asset. "Many times, with refinancing, the equity gained can be used to buy out the spouse's interest," he says. "There is a loan program out there for just about every potential homebuyer, regardless of credit history or lack of down payment."

Title Search Can Tell a Story

Dawn, a divorced mother of two, says she never knew a title search could tell so much about her home. She was 29 years old, with two young boys, when the divorce was final. The house was titled jointly to her and her ex-husband. The divorce decree deeded the house to her but she could not change the names on the mortgage. She was awarded a few hundred dollars a month in child support, but no alimony. The small amount of equity in the house was her financial security. She remained in the house for a year after the divorce and was able to make the monthly payments. She didn't know her ex-husband had chosen an adjustable rate mortgage at the time of purchase.

On the anniversary of the mortgage note, she received notice that her payments were about to double. She didn't earn enough to make the higher payment so she decided to sell the house, take the equity and find something affordable for her and her children. She listed the house with a realtor and sold it in two weeks, with closing set for 30 days after. She was happy to get her asking price so she would have some money to relocate, and she decided to bank the proceeds and rent an apartment until she found the right home for herself and her children.

Two weeks before the closing, her realtor called to say that a required title search uncovered two liens on her home from judgments recorded against her husband several years before. She had no idea judgments against her ex-husband could be held against her, but at closing she had to sign over all the proceeds to her ex-husband's creditors because their liens exceeded the available equity. She was left with no money and no way to buy a replacement home for herself and her children.

Just because you are deeded a house, don't assume you are getting any tangible assets. In hindsight, Dawn knows she could have avoided this problem if she had done a title search before accepting the house in the division of property.

Consider the attorney fees you incur battling over personal property. You don't want to pay $3,000 to fight over a $300 television. One hour of your lawyer's billable time will buy a lot of sheets and dishes.

CHAPTER 11

Personal Property:
She's Not Getting My Riding Lawn Mower

Personal property can be one of the most frustrating and hotly contested areas in a divorce settlement. By the time the parties divide the personal property, usually they have resolved the major issues in the case. You might be surprised how many cases that involve the custody of children and the division of large assets have broken down over relatively inconsequential personal property. Pride, ego and anger can cause people to fight over property they didn't even use during the marriage. For example, when the husband who does not cook, sew or entertain demands the wife's breakfast china and her sewing machine, the property division has become a punitive process and not a productive one.

The family feud over toaster ovens and lawn mowers gets so intense that some judges have ordered all the personal property sold and the money divided between the parties. This happens although recent precedents limit how far the trial court can go in selling the most basic personal property, such as clothing or toothbrushes. Any garage sale veteran knows the value received for used personal property is extremely discounted. The parties suffer financially if all the items are sold in this manner.

Potential Assets to be Divided

Personal property usually consists of the following:

- What each spouse brought into the marriage
- Property acquired by both spouses during the marriage
- Gifts and inheritances received by both spouses during the marriage (which may or may not be subject to division)
- Separate property purchased by both spouses during the marriage.

Often spouses agree on the division of property, but that doesn't mean they like the result. If the parties cannot agree, they can either have the judge divide it or come up with a plan for division of the disputed items.

If clients cannot resolve the division of certain items, we recommend what we refer to as the "kickball team" selection process. The parties flip a coin to determine who begins, and that party chooses one item of personal property from the disputed list. The other party then picks an item from the list and the process is continued in turn until all items have been selected. If one party wants to be punitive and select the other party's favorite item, the other party can return the favor with the next selection. The selection process remains balanced because of alternate selection. This can be done item by item or room by room, as the parties agree. Generally, if a case becomes bitter and combative, kickball team selection or the sale of all of the assets may be the only ways to resolve personal property issues.

Don't Fight Over Meaningless Personal Property

If the parties cannot divide the personal property on their own, a judge can do it. But judges do not have the time or the patience to quibble over personal property. The judge will not want to decide who is virtuous enough to merit the 27-inch television and who has to settle for the 19-incher. One Alabama circuit court judge cautions, "Unless

Numerous potential assets may need to be addressed in the settlement agreement. Any liabilities associated with these individual assets must also be addressed. The potential assets to consider include the following:

Artwork
Antiques
Automobiles
Bank accounts
Boats and Trailers
Business Equipment
Bonds
Checking Accounts
China, Silver, Crystal
Collectibles
401(k) Plans
Family Heirlooms
Fishing Equipment
Gun Collections
Home furnishings
Jewelry
IRAs
Life Insurance
Retirement Plans
Savings Accounts
Sporting Equipment
Stocks, options
Tools
Yard Equipment

there is no other way, I would not want to have a judge decide personal property issues. Our knowledge of the history and facts of the case is simply too limited. For that reason, I have become a strong advocate of mediation, where the parties can take more time to expand on a solution than a judge can in a trial setting."

Some judges require both parties to submit two personal property lists they consider a fair division of the personal property. Then they allow one party to select either list A or B provided by the other party. If the lists are not equal, the other side may pick the "better list" and leave the other party with the "bad stuff." At the same time, it may be impossible to create two equal lists due to certain favorite items. Either settle these issues to ensure you get your favorite chair or baseball card collection or spread these items out among two lists so that both contain desired items.

Fair market value is the price at which property would change hands between a willing buyer and a willing seller, neither one being under any compulsion to buy or sell, and both having knowledge of the relevant facts.

On the other hand, don't underestimate the potential tremendous value of the personal property. Often the sterling silver pieces that were given as wedding presents are now some of the most valuable assets in the home. Electronics and artwork and other amenities in the home can have significant value.

Factors the Court Considers

Many factors affect the division of personal property if the parties cannot reach agreement. Note that when the parties testify about dividing the personal property, it may not look good to the judge for one party to refuse to give even one item to the other spouse. The judge may ask the following:

- Who owns the property?
- Was the property owned prior to the marriage?
- Was the property purchased during the marriage?
- Was the property co-mingled during the marriage? (used for the common benefit of the marriage)
- Did either party contribute money or labor to the property?
- How long was the marriage?
- What are the parties' respective ages, health, occupation, employability and ability to be trained?
- What is the degree to which a spouse has diminished his or her future earning capacity because of years spent caring for children?
- What is the opportunity for each spouse to acquire additional capital, assets, or income in the future?

- What alimony payments will be made?
- What should each party equitably receive in the division?
- What is the fault of the parties?

Suggested Settlement Language

The settlement agreement may simply state that the parties divide the personal property and neither party makes any claim to the other's property. Or the agreement may contain a specific list of the property each party is to receive. If the parties are fairly amicable, you may be able to divide the household property without too much difficulty. If the situation is contentious, you may need to include a detailed list in the agreement. If the agreement states the wife receives half of the dishes, it may need to specify exactly which dishes. The assets may be owned in an odd number that cannot be evenly divided.

We recall one case where the opposing party attempted to claim that our client stole certain personal property. The agreement in that case stated, "the husband shall receive his tools." The husband claimed he had not received all of his tools. He supported his claim with a 15-page itemized list, which suddenly appeared after he claimed that he didn't get everything awarded to him. The wife said she had given him all the tools she knew existed. She didn't know whether he had the tools he was claiming, because she had never seen them. This type of conflict is fairly common with personal property division.

In that case, the husband spent more on legal fees to fight over these items than he would have spent to buy new tools. The memories associated with fighting over an asset can ruin any desire to have the asset after the divorce. The overall terms of the settlement agreement must be considered when determining whether it is worth fighting over personal property. The agreement may be tremendously favorable to you, and it may not be worth risking a less favorable result to go to trial over the couch and chairs.

The assets summary form below (Figure 3) allows you to list all the assets that might be subject to division in the divorce.

Asset Summary Form
Figure 3

WOOD & SHAW, L.L.C., ATTORNEYS AT LAW

Asset	Current Value (In Dollars)	Debt Amount (In Dollars)	Equity Amount (In Dollars)	Titled Individual/Joint	How Acquired

Even if one spouse
is the business owner, the
other spouse may have
an equitable interest.
This may come simply
from being
married to the other
person or from
"sweat equity" invested
in the business
by that spouse.

CHAPTER 12

Closely-Held Businesses

When the parties own a family business or some type of business ownership interest, it can be the largest asset in a divorce and a key element in the settlement. Determining which party controls the business and how the assets and liabilities of the business will be divided are essential to a successful breakup.

The way businesses are run can differ greatly. One spouse may operate the business or the parties may be jointly involved. Your business may be a small mom-and-pop operation or a multimillion dollar business with considerable assets and debts. Either way, the agreement should specify the resolution of all issues including the overall value of the business to the marital estate.

Who Owns the Business?

You must initially determine the legal form the business takes and who legally owns the business. The business may be in the name of one spouse, owned by both spouses, or owned by one spouse in a corporation, partnership, or joint venture with other people or entities. Some ownership interests are easier to divide than others.

Brad Sklar, a tax attorney with the law firm of Sirote and Permutt, says the parties should pay close attention to the form the business takes and the organizational documents. The court may order the sale, division or restructuring of the business to reach an equitable division of the marital property.

Types of Business Entities

The specific form of the business may affect its divisibility in a divorce. The business may have been held as one of the following:

- Sole Proprietorship
- General Partnership
- Limited Partnership
- C Corporation
- S Corporation
- Limited Liability Company (L.L.C.)

The following briefly describes these various types of business entities.

Sole Proprietorships

A sole proprietorship is the simplest form of business entity. This type of business is operated in an informal manner. It may be operated financially out of a personal bank account and physically from a desk in your extra bedroom. Generally, there is a single owner. The sole proprietor is responsible for all business debts and receives all the profit from the venture. Unlike a corporate structure where an owner may be able to limit personal liability, a sole proprietor cannot enforce such limits. At the same time, many sole proprietorships are tremendously successful businesses with a great deal of value.

General Partnerships

A general partnership can be formed with two or more individuals, corporations or limited liability companies. Under a general partnership, each partner is liable for the total debts of the partnership unless stated otherwise. The partnership documents generally address how the sale of all or part of the business is to be handled. These documents, which become important in case of divorce, sometimes include limitations on the sale of one partner's share or on transferring shares to another partner.

Each partner is generally responsible for income taxes on his or her share of the partnership income. If the partnership has losses, each partner may deduct a pro-rata portion of the loss. The amicability of the other partners can determine how easy it is to dissolve certain partnerships. Large or very complex partnerships have the potential to be difficult, if not impossible, to dissolve.

Partners sometimes make separate contributions and the current status of the business must also be taken into account. If the other partners do not have the desire or the capital to buy out another partner's share, it could mean that a spouse's partnership interest has little immediate value. In addition, the partnership interest a spouse would receive may simply involve the assignment and responsibility of the debts of the business. It may be unwise to take on that responsibility.

Limited Partnerships

A limited partnership is more specialized and structured and includes two categories of partners: a general partner and a limited partner. While the general partner has unlimited liability for the debts of the partnership, limited partners usually have no liability beyond the amount of their ownership. The general partner has expansive management responsibilities. A limited partner usually cannot have any management responsibilities or involvement in the day-to-day operation of the business and still maintain liability protection.

As a rule, therefore, the general partnership interest is considerably more broad in all aspects than a limited partnership interest. Being a limited partner in a business may give a spouse tremendous safety and financial security. It could also award a title that carries little or no authority to affect any change or receive any financial benefit.

Your lawyer should be able to examine the limited partnership documents to determine what interest is transferable under the limited partnership.

C Corporations

A corporation is a separate legal entity involving one or more shareholders. With a C Corporation, the business entity itself owes federal income tax on earnings. The corporation might be as simple as Bob's Taxidermy Service and involve one corporate shareholder. Or the corporation could be multinational, with publicly traded stock and thousands of shareholders. Generally speaking, the corporate shareholders of an adequately capitalized corporation are not personally responsible for the debts of the business unless they have provided personal guarantees. The corporate documents must be examined to determine what provisions are in place concerning the sale or division of the business.

The divorce court has the authority to award a spouse's corporate ownership to the other spouse. Most corporate documents specifically address what happens when one shareholder's interest is sold or transferred.

If the other shareholders own a majority of the stock and do not get along with the spouse who received the stock interest, you may not be able to control ownership of the company. In any corporate business structure, you need to have a clear understanding of the assets and debts of the business, as well as what the corporate documents provide, to determine whether this is an interest worth pursuing.

S Corporations

An S Corporation is perhaps the most common form of corporate entity for a closely held business. Generally, these corporations involve smaller corporate entities. Many times, a sole proprietorship is classified as an S Corporation for income tax planning and liability purposes once the business becomes more formalized.

With an S Corporation, the company's profits and income tax liabilities flow through to each individual stockholder on a pro-rata basis. The business entity does not pay federal income tax. This business involves one or more shareholders. Examine the corporate documents to see how a dissolution of the business is to be handled. If you hold a minority interest in the corporation and the corporation is not publicly traded, that ownership interest could be of little or no value. In fact, you could be taking on debt for a business that is floundering. But many S Corporations are extremely successful and a spouse's interest in the business might be valuable.

Even if your spouse doesn't value the business interest, other members of the business community may be willing to pay for it. If the corporate documents allow for the transfer or sale of your interest, you could receive tremendous value for it. Analyze the actual value of the corporation to determine if this is an interest worth pursuing.

Limited Liability Companies (L.L.C.)

A limited liability company (LLC) is a relatively new business entity that combines elements of a partnership and a corporation. It has the limited liability of a corporation but the tax aspects of a partnership. The liability of each member of the L.L.C. is limited to that member's individual investment in the entity.

Limited liability companies best illustrate the difficult task of melding a business into the asset mix of a marriage and equitably dividing those assets between the parties. If you have a company that makes and sells a very common type of widget, for instance, under many existing business forms you could easily divide the interest in that company. Certainly, one spouse or the other may have helped this company become successful, but you could see how the company might survive without that person. The situation gets more complicated if the company is based on a patent from the spouse or that person's unique training or education.

Many professional organizations, such as medical groups and law firms, establish limited liability companies for their practices. A professional such as a surgeon may own an interest in a limited liability company, but it would be impractical for the surgeon's spouse to own or control that interest. Usually, it is the surgeon's special skill that makes the medical practice valuable. Unless the surgeon's spouse can perform the same medical procedures, the spouse's interest is worth considerably less without the surgeon in the medical practice. In such cases, it's usually better for the spouse to receive more alimony on a monthly basis, or a greater share of the other assets, than a portion of the surgeon's share of the limited liability company.

Similar questions apply to all of the business entities described above. What interest, if any, would you receive? What is it worth? And what can you do with it? If the interest is not easily transferable, what other assets are available to compensate you?

All of these issues must be addressed in close detail with your legal counsel to determine what ownership interest is held in the business and what options are available.

Who Worked in the Business

Tammi Manley worked as a partner with her former husband in a very successful business. She believes it is important to look at each spouse's contribution to the business.

Many times in the early stages of a marriage, the spouse who is not the business owner works in the business or fills in during certain time periods. That spouse can be an actual employee or help out at the business without being paid. These considerations, known as "sweat equity," play a role in establishing your contribution to the business. Say you and your spouse agreed that you would build the business while your spouse raised children and did not work outside the home. The court usually feels the non-working spouse enables the working spouse to develop the business more thoroughly.

"Even though one spouse may not be listed as an owner or shareholder of the business, that person may provide considerable contributions to the business over time."

Business Owner Tammi Manley

What's the Business Worth?

More games are played with the value of a closely held business than almost any other financial aspect of divorce. One moment a business is providing lavishly for a family. Then divorce papers are filed. Suddenly the person who runs the business characterizes it as suffering a significant decrease in worth as a result of unforeseen market changes. Fast forward to when the divorce is over and ownership is settled. The business drastically increases its sales. For this reason, the actual financial records of each business must be closely examined to determine the accurate financial picture. Simply looking at tax returns may provide little or no useful income information.

The goal of most businesses and individuals is to pay as little tax as possible. The accountants for the business have a goal of structuring corporate information in a favorable light for tax purposes. Therefore, even though the business may not have much value for income tax purposes, it may be worth a considerable amount of money on the open market. The business may own assets and personal property that reflect a minimal value for tax purposes but, in actuality, have significant value.

It may be necessary to perform an audit of business records to determine what the business is worth. At a minimum, your lawyer should examine tax returns and other corporate documents, including profit and loss statements and bank records. You may have to retain an expert to perform a forensic audit of the business to determine its spending and value. For the purpose of equitable distribution, the following considerations are used to determine the value of the business:

- The nature and history of the business
- Tangible assets
- Earning capacity
- Fair market value
- Amount of goodwill
- Other intangibles

Perks and Other Benefits from the Business

In addition to income received from the business, examine the perquisites and other benefits received. For example, actual income received by the spouse may be minimal but the benefits may be significant. These benefits could include a company car, insurance payments, country club dues, retirement plan contributions, luxury travel, expense allowances, meal allowances, stock options, bonuses, deferred compensation and various other forms of compensation. All of these benefits may be perfectly legitimate income tax deductions, but they can also be considered income for divorce purposes. Simply because the IRS allows the business to deduct these expenses does not mean the divorce court cannot consider it as income. Contributions to 401(k) plans do not normally appear on a tax return, since they are paid from pre-tax income. As a result, the individual tax return may not reflect the total amount of retirement plan contributions made by one spouse or the respective matching contribution made by the employer. Even though one spouse deducts this money from gross income, it may be appropriate to count it for child support purposes.

Tax Liabilities of the Business

Even though the divorce agreement says the other party is responsible for tax consequences, the IRS may declare both of you responsible. If that happens, you may be required to seek relief from the divorce court and the specific language of the agreement will become critical. You may have little knowledge of the business operation or its tax history. Many spouses are shocked to find that they are going to be involved in an audit when the divorce is over. The IRS will look to both of you for taxes owed in a year when a joint return was filed. While sympathetic to the fact that a divorce has occurred, it may not waive your responsibility. This may not seem like a very big issue at the time of the divorce. But when audit or tax problems arise in the future, this issue must be addressed in the settlement agreement. The agreement should state that the responsible spouse will hold the other harmless for any future problems that relate to income tax liabilities.

"If you have been in business, handle your divorce like a business. Turn it over to a professional so emotions do not rule, but what's right and fair does rule."

Business Owner Tammi Manley

Under a Qualified Domestic Relations Order (QDRO), a retirement account can be divided between spouses with no immediate tax consequences.

CHAPTER 13

Retirement Accounts/ Stock Options

The great rush toward retirement has caused most Americans to emphasize tax-deferred investments. To soothe the fear of their employees that they won't have enough money to retire, many employers today match their employee's contributions. These generous programs create retirement accounts that can be the largest assets in a marriage.

If you amassed a substantial retirement account during the marriage, you may have to share it with your former love. Or you could be entitled to a share of your spouse's retirement plan in a property division, if you meet certain criteria. Generally, you must be married more than 10 years and the plan contributions must be made during the marriage. Typically, you can receive no more than half the value of the account.

Even if the individual retirement account is not subject to

division, the court can give you other property to offset the amount of your spouse's retirement account. For example, the court has the discretion to award one spouse equity in the residence equal in value to the retirement plan.

Although your current retirement benefits might not be worth very much, the plan may provide considerable benefits to be paid in the future. Determine the value of the plan at retirement.

The value of your plan at the time of the marriage is important to know because any increase in value during the marriage is marital property. One spouse may believe these increases belong to him because he worked while the other spouse was a homemaker. The court will not usually penalize the spouse who stayed home with the children by awarding the working spouse all the retirement benefits.

Verify that a spouse did not make substantial withdrawals from the retirement plan immediately before the divorce was filed. Someone planning a divorce for a long time may make significant withdrawals to reduce the value of the plan, and the use of any withdrawn funds should be analyzed.

To avoid tax consequences from dividing a retirement plan, enter a Qualified Domestic Relations Order (QDRO). A QDRO is a court order that requires the retirement plan to be divided, giving each spouse a share specified under the agreement or divorce decree.

Under this arrangement, the spouse who receives the share is not considered a plan member. He or she must adhere to the rules as they affect the spouse who owned the original account. For instance, the spouse who receives a share of the account may be older than the other spouse and expect to receive money from the account based on his or her own birthdate. But for purposes of accessing the account, the original plan member's birthdate controls such distribution.

Under a QDRO, taxes only occur when one spouse attempts to receive money from the account.

Meet with your accountant to determine the net value of the account if the money is utilized immediately. For example, a spouse not vested fully in the account may not receive all of the monies held in the account.

Survivor Benefits

Retirement plan survivor benefits may be applicable in the event of a spouse's death and should be addressed in a settlement agreement. A party may list his or her new spouse as the recipient of the survivor benefits.

There are usually specific language requirements that must be met concerning these survivor benefits. All retirement plans may not allow the transfer of these benefits. If this is a concern, consult your lawyer and examine what interests are available under the existing retirement plan.

Military Retirement Benefits

Military retirement benefits are especially complicated in case of divorce. If one party is entitled to military benefits, specific attention must be given to the language in the agreement concerning these benefits.

Asset Appreciation

While your house equity may be about the same amount as the value of a current retirement plan, one may have the potential to increase in value more dramatically than the other. Stock market growth during the 1990s doubled and tripled the value of retirement plans in a short time. Two decades ago, real estate was appreciating at a similar rate. Try to gauge the potential growth as well as the liquidity of each asset before deciding which one you want.

Can You Take Money Out of a Retirement Plan Early?

Whenever possible, avoid taking money from the retirement plan prior to retirement. Sometimes, though, raiding a retirement plan to pay off marital debts or settle a divorce can bring great peace of mind. Lump sum withdrawals made prior to the age of 59 ½ are generally subject to income taxes, as well as a 10% penalty tax. For example, if you take $25,000 from an IRA, you would pay a $2,500 penalty in addition to income taxes on the entire $25,000. But there are at least four ways to access retirement savings without being subject to the penalty for early withdrawal. Those methods are:

Section 72(t) transfer – This section of the tax code states that the 10% penalty doesn't apply to money withdrawn from a retirement account in substantially equal periodic payments. You could take monthly or quarterly payments, but you must take at least one payment a year for five years or until age 59.

Immediate annuity transfer – You can give money from your IRA, but not your 401(k), to an insurance company to fund an annuity that will pay you a specific amount of money each month.

Separation from service at age 55 – If money from a certain employer funds your retirement account, you can access that money without the penalty if you leave the job after age 55.

QDRO transfer to the spouse – This method is meant entirely for divorcing couples and is the easiest way to transfer retirement funds from one spouse to the other.

Can You Borrow Against Retirement Funds?

Under limited circumstances, you may borrow a portion of the vested interest in your retirement plan. Money borrowed against the plan is not taxed, provided it is repaid within five years. If the loan is not repaid on time, it is subject to income taxes and a 10% penalty. However, this loan is not subject to income taxes and may be at a more attractive interest rate than a traditional loan.

Stock Options

Stock options are a fairly new employee benefit that can provide substantial assets for distribution. More than one-third of large companies in this country now have broad-based stock option plans covering employees, consultants and outside contractors. This is more than double the number that existed in 1993.

Saving Your Assets

Stock options are rights given the employee to buy a certain amount of company stock for a specified price at a certain time in the future. The purchase of stock options is essentially betting that a company will do better and its stock will increase in value. Options are given to motivate the employee to stay with the company and help it grow. If the company does well, the stock usually goes up and the employee stock options value goes up in turn. If you or your spouse have stock options, attention must be paid to when the options were received. You should know whether they are vested, which means they can be cashed in.

Some states consider stock options as income of the recipient for child support and alimony purposes. Even if stock options are not vested, the court may award the other spouse a portion of non-vested options acquired during the marriage. This is a very hotly contested area of the law that continues to be ripe for appellate review.

If stock options are present in your case, determine their present value. For example, options covering one thousand shares of company stock may have been awarded to an employee at a value of $10 per share. If the stock is now worth $50 per share on the open market, the options are worth $50,000 minus the option purchase price. In this case, that price is $10,000, leaving a value of $40,000.

A more complex example would include the fact that the options were granted before the marriage at the same $10 price. It's easy to find out that on the day the couple was married, the stock was selling at, say, $20 per share.

In this case, only the appreciation in value from the point of the marriage is marital property. That would make the value of stock options $50,000 minus the $20,000 value at the time of the marriage, or a net value of $30,000.

A financial planner should be able to provide you with some expert advice on the value of options on a current basis. Likewise, they can advise you about the value of stock options versus other assets.

"Some people in this situation (typically women) have no work experience. They don't know how to act in an office environment. They are starting from ground zero, and at their age they will never catch up."

Mary Wier, Certified Divorce Planner

CHAPTER 14

Divorces Late in Life

Under Alabama law, special consideration may be given to divorces that take place late in life or after many years of marriage. Divorces that occur after 30 or more years of marriage or between people age 60 and above are almost exclusively exercises in the equitable distribution of property. Few of these cases involve child support or visitation schedules because children usually are grown and have their own families. So most of the court's attention is drawn to a careful division of the marital estate. "The longer the parties have been married, the more difficult these cases become," says Certified Divorce Planner Mary Wier. She counsels many people who have been married for three decades or more before getting a divorce. Her clients in these cases are mostly the wives who stayed home to raise children while their husbands flourished in their careers.

"Women in these situations have few career assets," she says. "I don't mean just that they have no income, pensions or bonus plans. They may have been at home for 25 years."

Wier says that in such cases, you must project the cash flow available to the person by calculating the return on assets she may take away from the marriage, including portions of the home equity, her spouse's retirement funds, defined benefit plans, stock options and bonuses.

"From this initial accounting," Wier explains, "you can determine whether the woman should ask for permanent alimony or for enough of the marital assets to invest and live off the return."

Just because the wife wants the money doesn't mean she will get it without a fight. "Somewhere in that equation, there may be a man who believes that all those assets are his because he was the one who went to work everyday," she says. "He wants the flexibility to retire or start another family. And so with those two quite different mind-sets, you have the makings of a real dispute."

Financial planners typically believe you need 70% to 80% of your pre-retirement income to be a comfortable in retirement. But Wier says that varies with different income levels. Those in the lowest income levels, who live paycheck to paycheck, usually need 100% of their pre-retirement income just to pay basic bills. Wier says that in her experience, those at the top income levels are also locked in to the need for disposable income.

"It's a matter of expectations," she explains. " They believe many of the luxuries they have are necessities, so they are not particularly happy without them."

Wier's experience shows that middle class people who divorce late in life seem to adjust better to the situation. They have enough money to cover basic needs and the ability to adjust expenditures to accommodate variations in income.

The courts encourage both sides to reach an acceptable settlement rather than having one imposed on them. Judges will, in most cases, affirm the agreement the parties make. But the law makes available to the person who was married 10 years or more three asset categories.

Under Alabama law, periodic alimony is available primarily to people in these long-term marriages. This type of alimony can be paid for the life of the recipient. People who were married more than 10 years also can be awarded half of their spouse's retirement accounts.

The other benefits available to people from long-term marriages are under the federal social security program.

Social Security Benefits

Under Social Security Administration rules, a former spouse may receive a portion of the ex's benefits, even though they are divorced. Social security rules further provide that if both you and your former spouse are at least 62 years of age, were married for at least 10 years and divorced for at least two years, you are eligible to claim spousal benefits. If your former spouse claimed benefits before the divorce, the two-year waiting period was waived.

These benefits may be collected as soon as your former spouse is eligible, regardless of whether he or she is actually collecting the benefits.

If you remarry while you are collecting dependent benefits from your former spouse's work record, you forfeit the right to those benefits. However, you may be eligible to collect dependent benefits based on your current spouse's work record. Should you divorce again, you may either collect benefits from your second spouse's record (again, if you were married for 10 years) or return to collecting benefits from your first spouse.

An individual paying into social security can begin to receive benefits when they reach age 62. Many spouses nearing retirement age fail to realize they can receive social security or a portion of their spouse's social security in the future. At the same time, if a spouse has not paid enough into social security or has not been at a job where social security taxes were paid, there may not be any benefits available. Obtain a printout from the Social Security Administration telling you what benefits are available in the future, either for the individual or through the other spouse's plan.

If you want to determine what your benefits will be under social security, contact the Social Security Administration office in your area and ask for an up-to-date printout of your available benefits. Appendix 10 contains an example of the Social Security Information Request Form that can be obtained from your local Social Security office.

Check through your financial records at home. The Social Security Administration usually mails out a detailed printout of benefits available on a periodic basis.

Wood ◆ Shaw

"People who cohabit prefer to test a live-in arrangement before jumping into marriage. It is ironic that the Wisconsin study indicates people who live together before marriage are more likely to divorce than those who don't."

Sociologists Steven Lake and Ruth Feldman

CHAPTER 15

Cohabitation

The number of unwed live-in relationships has exploded over the past several decades. This development has created unique problems in family law as well as those areas of the law relating to contracts.

Between 1960 and 1998, the number of unmarried couples living together in America increased by almost 1000%. Unmarried cohabitation – the status of couples who are sexual partners, not married to each other and sharing a household – is particularly common among people in their 20s and 30s. About one quarter of unmarried women age 25 to 39 currently live with a partner. An additional quarter of the same age group lived with a partner at some time in the past. Over half of all first marriages are now preceded by living together, compared to virtually none earlier in the century. [8]

In a random nationwide survey of 13,000 people, two University of Wisconsin sociologists found that 44 percent had lived with someone of the opposite sex before marriage. And 58 percent who were recently remarried had cohabited between marriages. [9]

How Legal Entanglements Happen

There is much to criticize about the system of marital dissolution in this country. But it is far more organized than the mess two people find themselves in when they have no legal paper between them as a guide to breaking up.

What happens if one party, who is paying one-half or more of the rent, decides to leave and the other party is unable to pay for the residence? The rules get even stickier if the couple buys furniture together, shares a bank account or has a child.

Common Law Marriage

Alabama is one of 11 states (and the District of Columbia) that recognize common law marriage, [10] which is treated in family law very nearly like conventional marriage. If there is cohabitation and the parties have the legal capacity and intent to be married, the primary requirement for a fully recognized common law union in Alabama is that the parties hold themselves out to the public as married. They can do this in numerous ways, including:

■ Calling each other husband and wife
■ Introducing themselves to others as husband and wife

- Purchasing property as husband and wife
- Listing each other as a spouse in wills or insurance policies

In some jurisdictions, merely living together for a certain period of time establishes the relationship. In Alabama, there is no time requirement to common law marriage. Once established, a common law marriage has the same legal effect as conventional marriage. Disputes between common law couples are subject to the rules of matrimonial law. If couples do not go the common law route, their disagreements are not part of family law but are treated simply as contractual arrangements gone bad.

Children of the Unwed

These situations naturally get more complicated when unmarried people have children. While a written agreement can settle where your new sofa will reside after a breakup, judges look at the best interest of the children in determining where *they* will live. In 1986, more than one-fourth of the 14.8 million children in single parent households lived with a parent who had never married; and 800,000 kids were living with unmarried couples. [11] Many of these children are subjects of custody battles, conflicts over visitation rights and child support enforcement fights.

Proving Paternity is Essential

Statistics show over the years that children of unmarried unions receive far less child support than children from conventional marriages. In many cases, the fathers simply refuse to believe these are their children. Proving paternity is essential to getting child support in these instances. Several hundred thousand paternity cases are filed each year in this country. The number is growing in part because of new, high-tech methods of establishing parentage. In years past, blood tests could be used to prove that a man was not the father, but these tests could not establish to a certainty that he was the father. Today, DNA fingerprinting is being used to establish paternity to a probability of greater than 99%.

Men also use these tests to establish paternity and assert parental rights when the mothers fail to allow them to see and support children they believe are theirs.

Wood ◆ Shaw

"Credit counseling brought me peace of mind by stopping the harassing calls from the bill collectors. My credit score actually improved after following the agency's advice."

Denny, a former client

CHAPTER 16

Marital Debts:
Someone Has to Pay Them

Marital debts often are the most problematic area in a divorce. This is largely because everyone wants the marital assets and no one wants the debts. It's important to list all the debts of the marriage and who incurred them. You must identify the joint marital debts versus individual debts solely in the name of either the husband or the wife. And you must know the purpose of this indebtedness.

If the husband bought a big screen television that remains his property, chances are he will also be responsible for the debt. If the debt was used for family purchases or for the children's benefit, the court may divide that debt between the parties rather than imposing it solely on the person whose name is on the bill.

The following chart (Figure 4) assists in determining and apportioning debt. This chart should prove a starting point and through the discovery process you can accurately determine all of the debts.

Debt Summary Form
Figure 4

Name on Debt	Current Balance	Account #	Monthly Payment	Individual /Joint	Purpose of Debt

Credit History

Another good source of information is a credit bureau report. You may be amazed to find the number of debts listed in your name. Appendix 11 provides a sample credit report request form for your use.

As with other features of law, ignorance of debt is no defense. If the parties have been paying a joint credit card debt for several years and both spouses have been charging on that card, the court is not going to believe you didn't know about the debt. Tell your lawyer what debts you were aware of and those you did not know about and the reasons for both. Many spouses have incurred joint debts without their spouse's knowledge and this type of fraudulent behavior should be addressed before resolution of the divorce.

Only in very simple cases should you ever sign a settlement agreement that says each of the parties will pay the debts listed in their names. Unless you have done an exhaustive review of your credit history, you may not be aware of all the debts listed in your name. You may face a rude awakening when numerous credit card companies call on you for payment of debts you didn't know existed. Many spouses take out credit cards in the other's name. This further emphasizes the need to identify each and every debt of the marriage before the divorce is final.

A contentious spouse can often impact the other's credit rating during and after the divorce proceedings, and this possibility is often overlooked in the settlement negotiations. To reach a settlement, the parties may agree to divide the joint debts. Customarily, there is language that the responsible party will indemnify and hold the other harmless for the debt he or she assumes. Occasionally, the parties share the debt load and each party makes payments to specific creditors, pending the sale of an asset (the marital residence, for instance) and the application of those proceeds to reduce or pay off joint debt.

There are hidden dangers in either of these scenarios. In one case, a divorcing couple agreed to divide the responsibility for payment of joint credit card accounts, applying the proceeds from the sale of their home to those debts and to the joint loan on the wife's late-model car.

After the divorce, the woman tried to use her car as security to apply for a bank loan to consolidate her remaining debts and purchase bedroom furniture for her daughter. Even with her car as security, the loan was denied. She was classified as a high risk and advised that she would have to rebuild her credit.

Her husband did not make payments on the debts he assumed. Even though the debts were now satisfied – all showing a zero balance – a number of creditors had simultaneously reported past due or delinquent status on the accounts. Because of these reports, she had a negative credit rating and was able to secure financing only by paying high interest rates. She faced a long, uphill battle to restore her credit rating.

Impact of Bankruptcy on Joint Marital Debts

The threat of bankruptcy is always a potential mine field as it relates to joint marital debts. Your divorce settlement agreement may state that one party is responsible for the joint marital debts. But if that party files for bankruptcy without paying off the debts, certain creditors may turn to you for payment. The settlement agreement should state that the paying spouse holds the other spouse harmless and is responsible for any and all obligations of the debt. The filing of a bankruptcy petition after the divorce creates havoc for the party responsible for the debt and the specific terms of the agreement become very critical.

Case law holds that a spouse who declares bankruptcy to get out from under a debt can be ordered to pay a higher amount of alimony to the other spouse after the bankruptcy. It may be wise to reserve the issue of alimony pending payment of the debt obligations even if both sides have agreed that alimony will not be paid. Reserving the alimony issue allows you a safety net in case the paying spouse defaults on debt obligations. The best option is either to pay off any joint marital debts or take responsibility for paying them yourself as part of the settlement agreement. It would be better to receive a greater share of an asset and be responsible for insuring the debts are paid than to be stuck with the debt after a spouse has filed bankruptcy.

Ted Stuckenschneider, an attorney board certified in consumer bankruptcy by the American Board of Certification, says time is important when an ex-spouse declares bankruptcy.

"If you receive notice that your spouse has filed bankruptcy and there are obligations to pay, contact a bankruptcy specialist immediately," he says. "Certain rights are lost if you do not file an objection quickly. If you are the one filing for bankruptcy, list your ex-spouse as a creditor if you agreed in the divorce to pay certain obligations and hold the other spouse harmless.

"While child support, alimony and certain maintenance payments clearly cannot be discharged in bankruptcy, all property settlements are subject to a decision of the court," says Stuckenschneider. "If you retain an interest in an asset until the debt is paid by the surviving spouse, your interest may insure that the debt gets paid.

If you think about declaring bankruptcy or believe your spouse may do the same because of financial trouble, get the advice of a bankruptcy expert. Sometimes it is better to divorce before you file bankruptcy. Each case has to be assessed on its individual merits."

If this is a concern, speak with your attorney before the settlement agreement is finalized.

Factors Considered
in Apportioning Debt

The trial court may consider a variety of factors when addressing the responsibility for marital debts. These factors include the following:

- Whose name is on the debt
- Purpose of the debt
- Who retains the asset related to the debt
- Financial resources of the parties
- Agreements between the parties concerning the debt
- Overall property division
- Length of the marriage
- Fault of the parties

Alternatives to Bankruptcy

If divorce was fair, your income, assets awarded to you in the divorce and any support you may receive would combine to fully meet your monthly expenses. That is not always the case. Dividing a household that was barely making it into two single income households with mirroring expenses can quickly lead to the realization that, despite all best efforts, your means do not meet your ends. Compounding this situation with calls from creditors or collection agencies can quickly lead to thoughts of bankruptcy. However, there are alternatives to filing bankruptcy that can save your credit rating and put you back in control of your monthly expenses.

"Even clients with good financial means can find meeting

their monthly expenses to be far more difficult than they originally expected," says Brian Turner, a lawyer in our firm with experience in the financial planning industry. "Clients fear damage to their credit rating and want to avoid bankruptcy if at all possible. Thankfully, several options exist to give clients relief without resorting to the bankruptcy court."

Those options include second mortgages, equity lines of credit, consolidation loans and assistance from credit consolidation agencies. For clients who receive the marital residence or other real property, second mortgages and equity lines provide options that can consolidate several debt obligations into one payment, and may provide tax benefits.

Advice from a Victim of Uncontrollable Debt

A big problem in Dave's marriage was controlling debt. After the divorce, he decided to stay clear of it. He did not own a credit card for the next five years. If he could not pay cash for something, he did without. He established a budget and forced himself to stick to it. He kept up with his monthly fixed expenses and saved money as he could. This allowed him to remain debt free and know where his money went every month. It was only when he began to travel with his business that he applied for a credit card. At this point, he was ready to manage any debt and always paid off the balances as they came due. Make certain you gain control of your debt, as Dave did, to prevent a continuing spiral of accumulated debt after the divorce.

Some traditional lenders offer loans to consolidate your debts into one manageable payment at a reasonable interest rate.

Saving Your Assets

Talk with your personal banker for additional information. Avoid transferring balances between credit cards. While many cards offer teaser rates to induce such transfers, consumers often get caught rolling the debt between cards, incurring unnecessary finance and interest charges and managing an ever-increasing debt load.

Credit counseling agencies provide an additional alternative if traditional lending options are not available. The Consumer Credit Counseling Service (CCCS) is a non-profit organization dedicated to helping people solve credit issues. For people with severe troubles, the CCCS debt management program allows you to repay debts by restructuring your budget and negotiating with creditors. There are more than 1,000 CCCS offices throughout the United States, Puerto Rico and Canada providing low-cost or free services.

Most creditors are happy to work with CCCS and other groups to ensure that obligations are satisfied. Creditors often reduce interest and finance charges once you enter a CCCS program. You make one monthly payment that is typically less than payments you made to individual creditors. Plans can pay off your outstanding obligations in as little as three years, a substantially shorter time than if you made only the minimum monthly payment on the same obligations.

As with any financial matter you undertake with your divorce, discuss the ramifications of these various alternatives with your attorney, financial planner and accountant before taking any action to insure you are following the wisest course for your financial situation.

Wood ◆ Shaw

Figure 5

Child Support Expenses	
Wood & Shaw, L.L.C., Attorneys at Law	
CHILD SUPPORT EXPENSES	MONTHLY PAYMENT/CHILD'S PORTION OF THE EXPENSE
FIXED EXPENSES	$
House payment	$
Insurance	$
Home	$
Automobile	$
Health Insurance	$
FLEXIBLE EXPENSES	$
Electricity	$
Gas or Oil (Heat)	$
Telephone	$
Water and Sewer	$
Cable Television	$
Pest Control	$
Yard Care	$
Repair/Maintenance	$
Other	$
FOOD	$
Groceries	$
Restaurants	$
Lunches	$
TRANSPORTATION	$
Car payment	$
Gas and Oil	$
Repairs/Maintenance	$
CHILDREN	$
Private School, Tutors, etc.	$
Activities (Sports, Music, Scouts, etc)	$
School lunches	$
Other school costs	$
CLOTHING/PERSONAL	$
Clothes - Children	$
Shoes	$
Cosmetics	$
ENTERTAINMENT	$
Sports, Movies, etc.	$
Vacations	$
Other Entertainment	$
EDUCATION	$
Tuition	$
Textbooks, Notebooks, Binders, etc.	$
MISCELLANEOUS COSTS/EXPENSES	$
Gifts (Birthdays, Holidays, etc.)	$
MEDICAL	$
Doctors	$
Dentists	$
Orthodontist	$
Optometrist	$
Medicine/Prescriptions	$
Other	$
OTHER	$
TOTAL	$

PART THREE

Details of the Divorce: Providing for the Future

Child support is for the children, not the custodial parent. It must be paid in nearly every case (provided the party has an income) and cannot be waived, even with a parent's consent.

CHAPTER 17

Child Support

In 1987, the Alabama Legislature adopted child support guidelines to standardize calculations. Before the guidelines were enacted, child support was not calculated uniformly and sometimes was waived in certain cases provided other payments or debts were paid.

The guidelines that determine how much child support is paid are based on a formula that considers the monthly gross income of both parents. Only in extreme conditions, such as when the noncustodial parent incurs significant travel expenses to see the child or pays an inordinate proportion of the child's expenses outside the court system, will a court consider a deviation in child support.

See the support guidelines at Appendix 16 to estimate what child support will be in your case.

How is Child Support Calculated?

The child support guidelines contain a chart similar in format to the Federal Income Tax chart that increases with the income of the parents. Under the guidelines, both parents' gross monthly income is totalled and the support is calculated on a pro rata share of that figure. The payment increases as the number of children increase. However, the payment does not increase an equal amount for each child. The custodial parent's day care expenses are also calculated as well as the health insurance costs related to the children. A parent can receive a credit against child support by paying health insurance premiums.

Day care expenses are limited to the Department of Human Resources' recommended guidelines per county. Generally, these numbers do not meet the cost of day care in large metropolitan areas of Alabama. Accordingly, these numbers may be considerably less than the cost of your actual child care. If so, the custodial parent may be responsible for most of this expense unless there is a variation in the agreement with the noncustodial parent.

What Expenses
Does Child Support Cover?

Child support is intended to cover the noncustodial parent's portion of ALL the child's expenses. In reality, this amount usually covers only the basics. If children are involved in extracurricular activities such as dance, piano, football, baseball, and other activities that incur significant fees and equipment cost, child support may not cover everything. However, the law provides only that the noncustodial parent pay child support under the guidelines, realizing that the custodial parent pays the difference. Extraordinary extracurricular expenses must be addressed in the agreement. Even if the other parent agrees to pay these expenses, you cannot eliminate the possibility he or she will later file a modification to the child support agreement asking to pay only according to the guidelines. With extracurricular activities, specific protective language must be included in the agreement. This language should state that the payment covers certain needs of the children and the reasons concerning the payment of such activities.

When Stephanie divorced 13 years ago, her children were in preschool and were not involved in many outside activities. Once they started school and began to be involved in sports and other activities, Stephanie was faced with additional costs. She paid fees and bought uniforms, shoes, pads, bats, gloves, helmets, and other equipment necessary for the sports her boys played. This cost was not included in the divorce decree or calculated as part of her ex-husband's obligation. Child support went for living expenses and was never enough to meet these added obligations. When the opportunity arose for her boys to attend summer camp, she had not included anything in her divorce decree about the boys' dad helping with that expense. She now wishes she had considered this at the time of her divorce. According to Stephanie, it was always too emotionally draining to ask her ex for any more than he was obligated to contribute and too costly to amend the divorce decree.

The vast majority of divorced people with children are reasonable about the children's needs and expenses. In a minority of cases, though, child support and payments for sports fees, clothing, tutoring, and even medical care are used as bargaining chips. Parents like these link child support to the frequency of visitation. The spouse paying support often believes the money is used extravagantly or to benefit the ex and not the children. The recipient spouse often complains about a lack of support and how the ex is spending much more on his or her new lifestyle or family. Under the law, though, child support is the only payment required from the noncustodial parent. Many noncustodial parents do much more, taking their children shopping and paying for extracurricular activities during the time they spend with the children.

Sometimes, when a noncustodial parent sends money for these expenses, the custodial parent tells the children he or she is paying for these activities. As a result, the noncustodial parent may be unjustly criticized for not paying over and above the child support guidelines.

Many noncustodial parents want the opportunity to take the children shopping and sign them up for sports and other activities.

Income That Exceeds
Child Support Guidelines

The child support guidelines are based on a maximum combined monthly gross income of $10,000 per month. If the parents make more than $120,000 per year in combined gross income, the guidelines don't apply and child support is based on the needs of the child. Many dual-income families gross more than $10,000 per month. Obviously, there is a huge difference when the combined monthly gross income is $12,000 per month versus $250,000 or more per month. The court has no specific formula to determine the needs of children when the income is so large. In these cases, the courts consider the actual needs of the children. For example, if the children enjoy a luxurious lifestyle and have always gone to exclusive camps and schools, the court is likely to continue this type of lifestyle if enough income is available. It is important to document the children's lifestyle and spending requirements.

Needs of the Children

Every divorcing parent should consider the needs of the children when support issues are considered. This is critical when the parties' monthly gross income exceeds the child support guidelines, but it should be considered in every child support case. Keep in mind that the judge in your particular case probably has children or has been involved in enough child support cases that he or she is reasonably familiar with ordinary expenses. Prepare a budget including the expenses you incur for your children. The sample child support budget (Figure 5) should help you specify certain expenses. Documentation should accompany each of these expenses, to make certain you are using true numbers. Cancelled checks, bills and receipts or some other form of documentation can validate these expenses.

If the children attend public school, it may be difficult to verify expenses incurred on their behalf, even though a tremendous amount of money may be spent on them. This analysis almost always involves a self-audit of your spending. Several major areas to emphasize in your analysis include groceries, extracurricular activities, clothing, medical expenses, camps and tutoring or educational expenses. Many clients also include a portion of their housing and automobile expenses. This is especially true when the parent lives in a certain area so the children can attend school there.

Utilities and housing expenses are higher when several children reside in the house than when a single parent lives in a small apartment or home. However, judges in Alabama are split about whether they will reimburse the custodial parent for housing expenses.

The argument frequently heard against including these expenses is that the noncustodial parent is helping the housing investment of the custodial parent increase in value by paying toward their financial obligation. This is a hard argument to make if the custodial parent lives in the original home of the marriage and has not upgraded the housing expenses tremendously. Obviously, if the housing expense at the time of the divorce was $1,500 per month and now it is $3,500 per month, the noncustodial parent's argument against the increased support becomes stronger.

If your income for child support calculations exceeds support guidelines, financial records and expense documentation will be necessary to prove your case. The court needs to know about the lifestyle of the children prior to the divorce. Spend time developing your budget and go over it in detail with your lawyer.

Unemployed or Underemployed Spouses

If the parent paying child support is unemployed, he or she may not have to pay child support at that time, depending on the reasons for the unemployment. If the payor spouse has been unemployed for some time due to unforeseen circumstances such as an injury or plant closing, the court may reserve the issue of child support until another time. Reserving an issue means the court retains the right to address the issue in the future. If the judge believes that person is voluntarily underemployed or is not trying to get a job, the court can require child support payments even though the spouse is not actually earning an income. This kind of forced participation is necessary in some cases. Otherwise, a spouse might simply claim disability or not work at the time the child support was calculated to avoid the obligation.

Overtime pay often affects child support. Even though the payor spouse has received 20 hours of overtime each week for the last 10 years, that spouse may argue child support should be based solely on a 40-hour workweek. The court typically averages the last three years of overtime and utilizes that figure. It is important to have income figured to support overtime as well as the payor spouse's employment records.

If the payor spouse has been working a tremendous amount of overtime to benefit the family, the judge may not impose such a demanding schedule if the other spouse has left and moved away with the children. One case recently held that a spouse who had taken a job making less money could do so based on the actual reasons surrounding the job change. These cases are considered one at a time and the payor spouse needs to prove the reasons concerning the change in income. The parent receiving child support needs to prove the payor spouse is capable of making additional money or continuing to work overtime.

Income Withholding Orders

An income withholding order (IWO) can be entered to withhold child support directly from a spouse's paycheck. Income withholding orders are now entered automatically, unless the parties have reached an alternate arrangement to pay the custodial spouse directly and the court approves the alternate arrangement. If the payment of child support is a concern, the income withholding order simplifies the process. If the payor has been actively involved in the care of the children, he or she may prefer that the employer not be forced to generate a separate check due to privacy reasons or a perceived stigma associated with an IWO.

IWOs really are becoming more common today. Because they are so common, they don't really reflect negatively on the payor spouse. If the parents want to work together, or if the payor spouse has a strong desire to make the support payment directly, the court will enter the IWO but not serve it on the payor spouse's employer. Then if the payor becomes delinquent in his or her child support obligation, you can file a motion with the court to enter the IWO. Do not hesitate to request the IWO at the first sign of problems. There can be significant delays associated with this process.

Post-Majority College Support

Alabama is one of the few states that require post-majority college support. The age of majority in Alabama is 19 and child support must be paid until the nineteenth birthday unless children marry or become self-supporting. Post-majority college support can be awarded beyond the age 19 to pay specific college and other education related expenses, such as tuition, books, room and board and fees. The parties can agree to other items such as fraternity and sorority expense allowances and automobiles, but the court usually will not require a parent to pay for these items.

Tuition expenses are based on in-state tuition at public schools such as the University of Alabama or Auburn University. Scholarships are normally credited against these expenses. Child support does not continue in addition to college support. Instead, the custodial parent is limited to paying specific college expenses. If college support begins before children turn 19, child support usually is modified.

Most settlement agreements specify that one parent will pay all the college expenses or that the parties will divide them in some pro-rata fashion. The court often reserves the issue of college expenses when parents cannot agree or the children are so young that college expenses are too far in the future. The custodial parent has the right to come back to court to ask for these expenses in the future. Unless the court reserves the issue, a formal request can be made to the court before the children reach age 19, even if college wasn't addressed in the agreement or is forever waived.

The court will consider the actual expenses of the college education and the scholastic aptitude of each child. If children have not chosen a college or don't know what the expenses are, the court may consider the application for college expenses to be premature. For children without the grades or test scores to qualify for college, the court may not force a parent to pay for a child who does poorly in school. Additional attorney's fees may be required to implement the request if you have to go back to court to address college when the time comes.

The college obligation usually continues until each child receives an undergraduate degree, but no longer than a specified time period from high school graduation. Usually, children must maintain at least a "C" average and be on track toward obtaining a college degree within a specified time period. The agreement usually stipulates that the payor spouse has access to grades and academic standing as well as course work and course selection. It can be extremely upsetting for a spouse to pay for a child majoring in "basket weaving" and not have any input into course work.

College support is a huge issue being hotly contested in a number of states on constitutional grounds. Many people feel that if a parent cannot be compelled to pay for college in an intact marriage, how can this be fair after a divorce? It is likely you will see this issue continue to be battled until a final resolution in the Supreme Court.

Child Support Payment History
Figure 6

The following chart (Figure 6) is very helpful in document-
ing child support payments in your case. These records should be
kept whether you are paying or receiving support. In a dispute,
information such as this helps you establish an accurate payment
history. It is also helpful to keep copies of the checks if a dispute
is likely to be based on the history of your case.

		WOOD & SHAW, L.L.C.			
		Privileged & Confidential			
		_____ V. _____			
		CHILD SUPPORT PAYMENT HISTORY			
Due Date	Date Paid	Amount Owed	Amount Paid	Balance Owed	Notes

Factors Considered by the Court When Making an Alimony Award

The court considers numerous factors when determining an appropriate alimony award. Each case must be decided on its own merits in conjunction with the overall property settlement. The court will usually consider the following factors in making an alimony award:

- The parties' financial resources
- The length of the marriage
- The respective age, health, occupation and employability of the parties
- The apportionment of property under the settlement agreement
- The degree to which one spouse has diminished his or her future earning capacity or education because of years spent caring for children or serving as a homemaker
- Standard of living enjoyed during the marriage
- Tax consequences of the awarding of alimony
- Fault of the parties in the breakup of the marriage

CHAPTER 18

Alimony

Few items cause more consternation in a divorce case than the possibility of imposing alimony. One side usually wants it and the other side will do almost anything to avoid paying it. The vast majority of alimony recipients are women. But if the woman is the main breadwinner in the marriage, the man could be eligible for alimony. The following summarizes the basic forms of alimony under Alabama law and the factors the court considers in making an alimony award.

Alimony in Gross

One spouse can make a single payment to the other as alimony in gross. This is usually part of the overall settlement and the settlement agreement must specify the amount. Alimony can be paid in one lump sum or in installments. Unlike periodic alimony, alimony in gross cannot be modified even if circumstances change in the future. This type of alimony is not taxable income to the recipient nor can the payor spouse deduct it. Certain forms of alimony in gross may be dischargeable in bankruptcy. That could be a concern if you receive alimony in installments.

Rehabilitative Alimony

Rehabilitative alimony is usually designed to be paid for a shorter period of time and help a spouse recover financially after a divorce. If one spouse has not worked in several years or just needs time to recover from the financial impact of the divorce, rehabilitative alimony may help. For example, one spouse may need additional financial help to complete a training program or until the children begin school. If rehabilitative alimony is utilized, the amount and length of the payments must be specified in the settlement agreement.

Periodic Alimony

Periodic alimony is usually awarded in marriages that last more than 10 years and is paid over a period of time. This type of alimony is paid for a specified length of time or until the spouse remarries, dies or cohabitates with someone of the opposite sex. Periodic alimony is taxable to the recipient and deductible for the payor.

Anyone receiving periodic alimony should meet with an accountant or tax professional to determine the net income after taxes, due to the tax consequences of alimony. Payor spouses should also meet with a tax professional to determine the advantages of making the alimony payment.

Periodic alimony can be modified in the future under certain circumstances. If the needs of the receiving spouse or the resources of the paying party change, either spouse can request a modification. Many paying spouses are shocked that their desire to seek other employment at a lower income or to work less is not an adequate reason to reduce alimony. Some parties have misconceptions about periodic alimony. Many mistakenly believe they are entitled to receive periodic alimony regardless of the length of the marriage, the parties' financial resources or the fault of the parties. In reality, financial resources usually determine whether periodic alimony is possible.

If the debts and obligations of the parties result in a negative cash flow for the payor spouse, the court is not likely to award substantial alimony despite the needs of a spouse. In long- and short-term marriages, however, the court may award considerable periodic alimony when financial resources are adequate. This is especially true when the payor spouse is responsible for the breakup of the marriage.

When periodic alimony payments are valued over time, an alimony award can be valued from several hundred thousand dollars to as much as several million dollars. Periodic alimony has extreme financial ramifications for both parties. As a result, most payor spouses will try everything possible to avoid periodic alimony while most receiving spouses usually do everything possible to ensure such an award.

If the recipient of periodic alimony gets remarried or lives with another person of the opposite sex, periodic alimony may terminate. If you are set to receive alimony, consider whether you plan to remarry in the near future. If so, it may be better to negotiate for more assets and not battle over a long-term periodic alimony award.

Sometimes you can modify the alimony award even if it specifies a length of time. Very specific language is required in the agreement to limit the periodic alimony to a certain number of years or months. Without this language, it may be possible to modify the agreement. To limit the periodic alimony to a specific number of months, the settlement agreement must state that the parties do not intend for it to be modifiable in the future and that the agreement represents an integrated bargaining agreement.

Our firm was involved in a case that successfully went to the Alabama Supreme Court concerning alimony modifications. In that case, a husband agreed in his divorce to pay periodic alimony for 10 years, with his wife receiving the majority of the marital assets. He did this with the expectation that after 10 years, he could end the alimony payments and begin to save for his retirement. In the ninth year, the ex-wife petitioned for an extension of the alimony.

The husband hired our firm to defend the modification and after a two-year battle, the Alabama Supreme Court affirmed the husband to have an integrated bargaining agreement that could not be modified. However, the client had to endure two years of litigation and significant costs to avoid the modification.

The language in the agreement may not guarantee that terms cannot be modified, but it certainly will work against a modification.

Tax Consequences of Alimony

There are specific tax consequences associated with each type of alimony being paid. Alimony in gross is generally non-taxable to the recipient spouse and nondeductible to the paying spouse. Periodic alimony is taxable to the recipient spouse and deductible for the paying spouse. Therefore, the actual value of the award and the cost of the award to the paying spouse may be significantly affected by the tax consequences. Anyone receiving or paying alimony should consult with a tax professional to determine the cost or value of the alimony award.

Alimony and Bankruptcy

Spouses paying certain forms of alimony may be able to rid themselves of the obligation through bankruptcy. Of course, this is bad news for spouses who receive alimony over time. The bankruptcy laws have specific applications for alimony payments and the issue of dischargeability must be addressed in the settlement agreement. Periodic alimony generally cannot be discharged in bankruptcy, while alimony in gross often can be. Bankruptcy may affect terms of the divorce agreement. It can drastically affect your rights under your divorce agreement. If you think your spouse may file bankruptcy, you need to address this concern with your attorney because protective language may be able to assist you in limiting the potential damage of the bankruptcy down the road.

For example, your spouse may attempt to discharge past due alimony payments. To protect yourself, the original settlement agreement may provide some security, such as a lien against a piece of real property or other security to limit the payor's ability to bankrupt.

Alimony Modifications

It may be possible to modify certain forms of alimony when there is a change of circumstances after the divorce. Either the payor spouse or the recipient spouse can seek a modification of periodic alimony. If the paying spouse becomes ill or has a reduction in pay due to legitimate reasons, the court will be more receptive to a modification than if the spouse has voluntarily decided to quit a high income job. In that scenario, the court may require the spouse to pay the original alimony amount even though his or her income has decreased. Generally, the largest issue of contention in this area is whether the decrease in income is legitimate. Many times these cases involve taking depositions of employers or personnel managers to determine whether the individual truly warranted a legitimate decrease in income.

If the payor spouse's income or assets increase dramatically, you may be able to increase the award. If the payor spouse is involved in a job the other spouse supported during the marriage, the former spouse may share those dramatic pay hikes through an increase in alimony.

Alimony Payment History
Figure 7

The following chart (Figure 7) can help you document alimony payments in your case. These records should be kept whether you are paying or receiving alimony. When a dispute over payment arises, this information will present an accurate payment history. It is also helpful to keep copies of the checks if a dispute is likely, based upon the history of your case.

WOOD & SHAW, L.L.C.
Privileged & Confidential
_____V._____
ALIMONY PAYMENT HISTORY

Due Date	Date Paid	Amount Owed	Amount Paid	Balance Owed	Notes

The trial court usually awards tax exemptions to the custodial parent. The parties may agree to divide or split the exemptions, alternate them each year or claim at least one child each if there are two or more children involved.

CHAPTER 19

Overall Tax Consequences

Tax issues are often overlooked and can haunt you for years after your divorce is final. There may be issues related to the sale or division of an asset. You may owe capital gains taxes on the sale of a marital residence or other asset. You may face tax consequences associated with retirement plans, alimony and other financial matters, including the dissolution or sale of a business. Many parties fail to realize the impact of taxes on their settlement agreement until after the court has approved it. At that point, the tax burden may exceed any value received under the agreement. You may begin to think about tax consequences only after you have received a letter from the IRS, months or years after the divorce, notifying you of an audit. If you are involved in a case with significant assets or large incomes, make certain you and your lawyer address the tax consequences associated with every facet of the agreement.

The following is a brief summary of the most common tax consequences facing divorced people. This should be considered only as an introduction to the tax issues discussed. The Internal Revenue Code and related cases are extremely complicated and you need to seek specific advice concerning the issues involved. Appendix 1 contains a list of accountants throughout the state who can provide assistance to you related to personal income taxes as well as business tax issues. This list of accounting professionals is a starting point to lead you to a professional who can assist you in your particular case.

Current Year Tax Returns

While married couples typically file joint tax returns, divorced spouses must file separately, often leading to higher tax brackets and larger tax burdens. There may be significant tax consequences associated with filing jointly or separately for a particular year and the timing of a divorce decree may be important. If a divorce is final and the order entered before December 31 of any year, the parties must file separate returns for that year. If you wait until after December 31 for the final decree of divorce, the parties can agree to file joint returns. Usually, one party is responsible for any tax liabilities associated with that return.

Tax Consequences of Payments and Transfers

Besides changing your filing status, the financial division and physical separation associated with a divorce can create significant tax consequences to the parties involved. Alimony payments often are deductible for tax purposes by the payor and result in taxable income for the recipient. Child support payments, on the other hand, do not constitute taxable income for the recipient spouse.

Property transfers from one spouse to another are treated as gifts. Neither party has a gain or loss for income tax purposes on this property. The transferee's tax basis in the asset is the transferor's adjusted basis immediately prior to the transfer. Where the parties are in different marginal tax brackets, you might consider a transfer of marital property where there is a larger built-in gain to the spouse with the lower tax bracket. You could transfer marital property with little or no gain, or that may have actually declined in value, to the spouse in the higher tax bracket.

Say that a divorcing couple has divided much of their property equally. All that's left are a lake house and their stock portfolio. The value of the stock is approximately the same as the equity in the house. Giving one person the stock and the other person the house may seem equal except for the fact that the husband, who is retired, is in a much lower marginal tax bracket than the wife, who still works. Depending on how long they have owned these assets, the lake house may create a greater tax burden because of capital gains. As you see, these property arrangements are so complex and subject to so many variables that you need to check them out with a tax expert.

Prior Tax Liabilities

The settlement agreement should state which party is responsible for prior tax liabilities in the event of a deficiency, even if that deficiency is not discovered until after the divorce.

The IRS may audit a prior tax year when the parties filed a joint tax return. Taxpayers filing jointly are each liable for any tax, interest or penalties associated with that return. The agreement should specify who is responsible for any deficiency found in the future. The responsible party should be required to indemnify the other party if that other party is forced by the IRS to pay that tax liability. Regardless of who is deemed responsible in the settlement agreement, the IRS can collect any amount due from either or both parties. Many times a spouse simply signs a joint tax return and does not know what information, correct or incorrect, is contained in the return. While the IRS can collect from either taxpayer, the "innocent spouse rule" may give relief to a qualifying spouse who had no knowledge of the other side's understatement of tax on a joint return.

Capital Gains Taxes

Assets sold as a result of the divorce can create capital gains for which taxes are owed. The most common asset to which this applies is the marital residence. Any appreciation received in the home since its original purchase date may be subject to capital gains taxes. The impact of these taxes should be addressed before the case is resolved. Recent changes to the tax code broaden the amount of gain exempt from capital gains tax, but this is an area where timing can be critical and a misstep can be punishing. Factors that have significant impact on capital gains tax liabilities are whether the home is a principal residence, whether one spouse was granted sole use of the home in a divorce instrument and the timing of the other spouse's departure from the home. You may avoid tax consequences on the equity in the residence, provided it is transferred into another marital residence or certain other requirements are met. As a result, you should consult with your lawyer and your tax professional concerning these issues before resolution of your case.

Tax Exemptions

A taxpayer may claim a personal tax exemption for any qualifying dependent. Children under the age of 19 almost always qualify as dependents. The child support guidelines as well as the IRS assume the custodial parent is awarded the income tax dependency exemptions for any children.

CPA Tim Downard says most divorce settlements allocate dependent exemptions and the related child tax credit. If the noncustodial parent receives the tax exemptions, it is generally considered a deviation from child support guidelines and may warrant an increase in child support to the custodial parent. Sometimes, though, the tax exemption may provide little or no benefit to the custodial parent. It may be more economical for the noncustodial parent to receive the tax exemption. If the custodial parent is not working, for instance, there is usually no need for that parent to receive a tax exemption that would provide no benefit on tax returns.

The IRS requires Form 8332 (see Appendix 9) to be filed concerning the tax exemptions after the divorce. This form may satisfy the IRS concerning the exemptions in the future. If both spouses claim the children, the IRS usually rejects both tax returns, since its computer database is designed to spot duplicates.

Retirement Plan Issues

Dividing a retirement plan as part of the settlement and avoiding tax consequences may be possible by entering a Qualified Domestic Relations Order (QDRO) or by one of the methods detailed in Chapter 13. A QDRO basically divides a single plan into two plans, leaving a portion in the name of the original owner who participated in the plan and transferring the remaining portion into the former spouse's name.

If one spouse withdrew a significant amount from the retirement plan during the divorce or prior to the separation, the settlement agreement should say which party is responsible for tax consequences associated with the withdrawal. Many parties conveniently make a significant withdrawal from their retirement plan immediately before filing for divorce. If the parties have agreed to file joint tax returns as part of the divorce agreement, the responsibility for income taxes associated with that withdrawal should be addressed on the forefront.

On the other hand, transfer of an individual retirement account (IRA) or an individual retirement annuity pursuant to a divorce is not a taxable transfer and no QDRO is necessary to divide or transfer an interest in an IRA.

Overpayment of Income Taxes

A clever and often-used way for a spouse to hide significant income is by overpaying income taxes for the future year. For example, if the person was due a significant income tax refund and applied it to next year's tax liability, funds may be missed during settlement of the case.

Make certain your spouse has not significantly altered his or her income tax withholding. In this way, he or she may receive a lower net paycheck with the anticipation of getting a tremendous return at the end of the year. One spouse might overpay taxes to reduce the value of a business for purposes of the divorce. This is discussed in greater detail below.

Taxing Closely Held Businesses

Many parties often report little or no personal income from their business on personal tax returns. Close examination of business tax returns and records related to the business, however, may indicate that the owner is receiving much more money and benefits. This may create IRS audit problems down the road as well as uncover considerable income the other spouse may need to resolve the case. An amazing number of businesses report little to no income for the years before the divorce, even when the family's household expenditures are extravagant each and every month.

Address the tax liabilities associated with a business and also sources of income a party may be receiving from a business. The IRS may allow a business to take deductions that are appropriate for tax purposes. But the divorce court may consider these deductions as income to a particular spouse. They include retirement plan contributions, company cars, insurance benefits, travel benefits, travel reimbursements and personal expenditures made by the company on behalf of an individual. Your accountant and other necessary professionals should consider the various problems associated with your closely held business. The IRS may eventually come knocking on your door and you need to make certain your settlement agreement includes as much protective language as possible.

CPA Randy Whirley says anyone getting a divorce should approach the situation like a business deal. "Do not let emotions get in the way of solid financial decisions that will impact you for many years to come," Whirley says. "Obtain all the information you can and invest in professional advice. Your investment in professional services will pay for itself in the long run. Remember that no two financial situations are exactly the same. The level of wealth, revenue, economic conditions and political environment can and will change. The best course of action is to construct a well-conceived financial strategy."

"One of the most common tax-related problems is the failure of self-employed individuals and other small businesses to properly report all taxable income or simply pay the tax liability shown on the joint return."

Tim Downard, CPA

Wood ◆ Shaw

You may be required to maintain hospital and major medical insurance for your minor children until age 19. Of course, if no health insurance is available, it may be difficult to force a party to obtain coverage.

CHAPTER 20

Health Insurance

If both parties can secure health insurance through their employment, this may be an easy issue to resolve. If one party does not work or has been covered on the spouse's policy, this issue needs to be closely examined. If there are minor children, the settlement agreement should address which party will provide them with insurance coverage.

Health Insurance for the Spouse

Most health insurance plans will not allow the employee/spouse to provide coverage for the other after a divorce. Dependent coverage usually is offered, but a former spouse is no longer a dependent. The spouse needing insurance coverage has the following options:

Coverage through his or her own employment

A spouse may already be covered or can enroll for coverage through an employer. This is often the easiest solution. If you seek employment after the divorce, take a job that provides insurance.

Coverage under COBRA
(Consolidated Omnibus Budget Reconciliation Act)

A party may be able to continue the same coverage that was available before the divorce under the former spouse's plan. This coverage is offered for a limited time under the federal COBRA program. Since COBRA coverage is limited to companies of a certain size with specific insurance plans, the spouse seeking this coverage should confirm that COBRA is available before the final resolution of the case.

Many agreements generically state that the spouse shall continue coverage under COBRA when, in fact, COBRA may not be available. Also, the premiums associated with COBRA are usually higher than those paid through the employer. The settlement agreement should address who will be responsible for COBRA premiums. The former spouse will have premiums associated with personal coverage, as well as any coverage for the children. In other words, COBRA premiums will not be included in the cost of the previous family coverage.

Obtaining coverage through an independent source

Individual coverage can also be obtained. Individual policies do not provide the best coverage and are usually priced higher than group plans. Address what the independent health plan covers and how much it costs. If there are high medical expenses, it may be wise for an individual to obtain employment where health insurance is offered rather than purchasing an individual policy that offers lesser coverage.

Pre-Existing Conditions

Federal law mandates that group health plans written through an insurance company cover pre-existing medical conditions under most circumstances. To avoid covering catastrophic conditions, some large employers have gone to self-insured plans that are not covered under the Health Insurance Portability and Accountability Act (HIPAA). If one spouse has a major health condition, such as heart disease or cancer, these non-HIPAA plans may not cover the condition after the divorce. The same goes for individual insurance coverage.

If the spouse getting the new insurance has a history of medical problems, it may be necessary to address the cost of these medical treatments in the divorce, if they are not going to be covered by insurance. Most self-insured and individual plans have a mandatory waiting period, sometimes up to a number of years, before pre-existing conditions become eligible for coverage. Group plans covered under HIPAA must include pre-existing condition coverage when the party can prove he or she had uninterrupted coverage under a group plan for the same condition for a specified period of time before the divorce. You can prove this coverage by securing a certificate of coverage from your previous insurance company.

Saving Your Assets

If pre-existing conditions affect your ability to get health insurance, look at whether your medical expenses will be covered under the new insurance. If expenses are not covered, you may need to re-examine your budget and include expenses for your projected medical care.

Many chronic medical conditions, such as cancer, involve lengthy treatment and can play a large role in your need for alimony, due to the medical costs associated with the illness. The illness may place limitations on your ability to work, increasing the need for financial support.

This type of health condition may be a very contested issue in your divorce. For example, one party may argue that the other spouse is not really sick and is exaggerating the illness to elicit sympathy from the court. To prove or refute this allegation, physicians may be called to testify about a party's condition and its impact, if any, on the ability to work. If this is an issue in your divorce, make your lawyer aware of your condition early in the case. Your lawyer will want to take a doctor's deposition to get expert testimony on the condition. This expert testimony can become very expensive in your case. But if there is a large amount of money at stake, you may have no choice but to engage such an expert.

Your lawyer can tell you whether the court will likely view certain medical conditions as sufficiently severe or significant under this type of alimony analysis. You can reduce unnecessary expenses in this regard. Simply asking for your medical records for the lawyer to review can save you money. If the lawyer's office has to subpoena the records, the doctor's office usually charges for copying the records. There also will be increased legal fees.

Health Insurance for the Children

Your settlement agreement should specify which party is responsible for medical insurance and how the parties will address any expenses that are not covered. Child support guidelines assume that the custodial parent pays the first $200 of non-covered expenses per child per year and the parties divide any amounts over that. Usually, one spouse is responsible for these expenses or the parties agree to equally divide them. There are often charges not covered by insurance, including copayments for doctor visits, hospital charges, prescription drugs, physical therapy, optical, dental, orthodontic or counseling expenditures. When a child is diagnosed with a major illness such as leukemia, these expenses can be monumental and potentially lead to financial difficulty for one or both parents.

Note that if the case is tried, the court will often require the parties to divide the cost of any expenses not covered by insurance. This is often done to prevent one parent from going overboard with medical expenditures when they are not liable for the costs. If both parties have a financial stake in medical expenses, they are more likely to be conservative in selecting treatment options.

Confirm that Insurance is in Place

Make certain health insurance is actually in place. This is best illustrated by the following example: In Dawn's divorce decree, her ex-husband was required to provide the children with health insurance coverage. She was told before the divorce the

195

name of the insurance company. So she called to confirm the coverage and ask about COBRA coverage for herself. She was told that her coverage did not satisfy company regulations. Their coverage was for employees who worked a minimum number of hours each week and Dawn's ex-husband did not qualify. He represented a product line manufactured by this company and did not meet their requirements for health insurance coverage. Dawn did not qualify for COBRA coverage and her sons had no coverage at all. Her youngest son had lost his hearing as the result of an illness and her new insurance coverage would not cover this costly pre-existing illness.

In the decree, her ex-husband was to provide health insurance for his children after the divorce. Two months after the divorce was final, she was relieved to receive cards that verified he had purchased insurance for the children. Still, she called the company to verify the plan. She learned they had been covered for only 30 days and that the policy had lapsed the month before and had not been renewed. Her children had no health insurance and she was forced to return to court to force her ex-husband to obtain the insurance and show ongoing proof of its existence.

Once she obtained permanent employment, she included her children on her company policy. She knew coverage would remain in place and that her children would be protected. Dawn came to us after her divorce, when it was too late to prevent many of these problems. She had to invest considerable time and expense to enforce what she thought was already in place.

Wood ◆ Shaw

Always insist on life insurance if your agreement calls for payments over time – for child support, alimony or the payment of debts. Even if the payor spouse is young and healthy, he or she could be hit by a bus.

CHAPTER 21

Life Insurance

When children are involved and child support and other expenses are addressed in the agreement, there should be adequate life insurance on the payor spouse to fund those obligations if that spouse dies. Traditionally, the parties are required to maintain a specified amount of insurance or keep the life insurance they had during the marriage. The settlement agreement should specify that a party required to maintain insurance should provide proof of its existence to the other spouse on a regular basis, beginning immediately, and verify that the amount has not been reduced or borrowed against during this time.

The insurance industry offers a wide range of products these days, but they fall within two basic types: term and whole life. Term life is the least expensive insurance available. It provides nothing but a death benefit for a specific number of years, while many different types of whole life have investment capabilities. If your major obligation is child support, you can expect the amount to be reduced or the obligation to end over time. In this case, decreasing term is the best option. This means that as the years go by, the amount of death benefit gets smaller. Decreasing term policies are relatively inexpensive and tend to get less expensive with the years as the face amount gets smaller.

By contrast, a whole life insurance policy can earn considerable cash value over time. Often, spouses fail to note this value with policies written during the marriage and they leave it on the negotiating table without consideration. If life insurance is in place in your case, find out whether the policies have any cash value. Ensure that your spouse has not recently withdrawn this money. The settlement agreement should also specify the beneficiary of the insurance.

You can add a layer of protection for children by requiring that a trust be established for life insurance proceeds. Under this type of trust, the payor spouse can specify that a trustee (often the former spouse or another family member) use life insurance proceeds for the benefit of the children. When the children reach a certain age, the trustee is usually required to release the proceeds of the trust.

"The failure to have a trust means the probate court must select a conservator to manage and use the money for the children," says attorney C. Fred Daniels. "The other parent is the person most likely to be selected by the probate court as the child's conservator, even though there has been a divorce.

"Conservatorships are cumbersome and expensive. Funds in

the conservatorship must be used each year to purchase a bond equal to 110% of the value of the assets. Every three years, conservatorship funds must pay for an accounting before the probate court. Investments are limited and do not include any of the often desirable, growth-type investments appropriate for children. Distributions for the benefit of the children require approval in probate court. Worst of all, in Alabama children attain their financial maturity at age 19. This means the children gain control of the money when their financial goals probably have not matured.

"The difference between a conservatorship and a trust is that you make the rules for the trust," says Daniels. "You pick who will manage the property. You can give flexible investment instructions. You can state how the funds are to be used and specify the age at which children take control. This is often an older age such as 25 or 30, when children have greater maturity and long-term goals."

Life Insurance for the Custodial Parent

Custodial parents should consider purchasing additional life insurance on their own life after the divorce to benefit the children. Many parents fail to recognize the need for additional life insurance to protect the children in the event of the custodial parent's death. Chris Dorris, a State Farm Insurance agent, recommends term life insurance, which can be inexpensive but provide a tremendous amount of coverage in the event of a premature death. "There are two important facts to consider when purchasing term life insurance," Dorris says. "First is the right amount of insurance. Multiply the death benefit by a realistic rate of return. For example, $500,000 x 7% = $35,000. This represents the annual income your children could expect to receive without using the principal. Look at how long the term rate stays the same. Most companies will give you level rates for 10, 20 or 30 years. Your children's ages will help you determine how long you will need the policy."

Estimated Life Insurance Costs

Your ability to obtain additional life insurance and the cost of that coverage depends on your age and health. Greg Canfield, principal at the Canfield Agency, says many people are underinsured without realizing that they could have more insurance coverage at a nominal cost. The following chart (Figure 8) supplied by the Canfield Agency estimates potential life insurance costs for a basic term policy. The cost increases with the amount of the coverage, but many times the increase is not drastic.

Projected Life Insurance Costs, Figure 8

Face Amount	Age 30	Age 35	Age 40	Age 45
$100,000	$ 11.74	$ 12.60	$ 14.24	$ 17.93
$250,000	$ 16.21	$ 16.43	$ 19.22	$ 25.46
$500,000	$ 25.67	$ 26.10	$ 31.26	$ 42.44
$750,000	$ 35.78	$ 36.42	$ 44.16	$ 60.93
Monthly premiums based on a female, non-tobacco user at preferred rates. Actual premiums may vary by company, medical underwriting and/or type of policy selected.				

Prove that Life Insurance is in Place

One client says when she was divorced, the decree ordered her ex-husband to provide life insurance on himself for the benefit of their children. He was to pay the premiums and keep the coverage in force. She depended on child support to meet ongoing living expenses. She knew how critical life insurance was. In the event of her ex-husband's death, child support payments would cease. She was very upset to learn one day that her ex-husband had not kept the insurance policy in force. Also, she could not gain any information on the policy because she was not listed as the owner. At the time of her divorce, she should have been listed as the owner of his policy for her children. That would have allowed her to contact the insurance carrier and obtain information. Prove the policy is in place and insist that this proof be available on a regular basis. This helps you assure that coverage stays in force for your children's protection.

Advice from an Insurance Professional

Insurance salesman Robb Schiefer says many people are hampered by a general lack of knowledge regarding personal insurance forms, the purpose of the respective forms and the inherent intricacies of the policies. For example, most homeowner's policies limit jewelry coverage to a total for all items in the household of $1,000 to $2,500.

"The basic definition of insurance is 'the transfer of risk,' where risks relative to an individual's circumstances should be assessed," he says, "and the appropriateness of transferring that risk to an insurance company evaluated."

Before attending a trial,
review the facts of your
case. Each hearing is
important, and you and
your lawyer should be
prepared. Go through
the steps of the hearing
and understand
the relevant issues.

CHAPTER 22

Following Court Procedures

In Alabama, divorce-related matters are handled by circuit courts. Judges rather than juries decide virtually all divorce cases and post-divorce modifications. In the major cities of our state, certain courts are designated to hear only family issues involving juveniles.

In Jefferson County, for instance, three circuit court judges hear divorce cases. Four judges hear all family court matters in the county (including the Bessemer cutoff). The system works differently when you live outside the major cities. Circuit courts in the smaller counties decide a variety of cases, from divorce to criminal cases and other civil suits. There are advantages to both kinds of judges, but it is critically important to know what kind of court will be handling your case.

Temporary Hearings

A number of temporary matters set the ground rules, an important first step in the divorce process. From the time the divorce is filed, you and your spouse must try to decide how the house will be handled, how much child support or spousal support will be paid and what will happen to certain assets and bills before the divorce is final.

In most instances, these issues are settled between the parties or their lawyers. A phone call or two puts the process in motion. Sometimes parties become very creative at this time. For instance, if they can't decide who stays in the home, we've seen people agree that the children should stay in the home and each parent should alternate weeks living with them. This does not work in many cases, but who's to say that it can never work.

Only in the most contested cases should you have to resort to a temporary hearing to resolve these matters. Temporary hearings are expensive and time consuming but may be necessary if the parties cannot agree. In counties that have specialty courts, special masters handle many divorce-related pre-trial activities. These special masters assist the judges. In the jurisdictions that don't employ special masters, the judges themselves decide temporary issues.

Preparing for Trial

Those who come to divorce court the most prepared have the best chance of winning. This principal extends from the preparation of witnesses and your theory of the case to the way you look and act. Once your attorney becomes familiar with all the finan-cial information relevant to your case, it is important to review the entire case prior to trial.

Each hearing affects the eventual outcome of your case. You and your lawyer should review what will happen in the hearing and the relevant issues that need to be addressed by your side. Your counsel may even request that you attend a trial similar to yours so that you can get a good idea of the intensity of the pro-ceeding and what to expect from the opposing counsel and the judge.

In many cases, your lawyer will prepare you for the hearing by running through questions that might be asked in court. Probably more important than what you are asked is how you answer. There are many ways to truthfully answer the same ques-tion, and you must rely on the experience of the attorney to let you know the proper way to reply.

Just Answer the Questions

Your attorney should know how much information the court needs to make a decision. Many clients want to tell the judge minute details of the marriage. A good lawyer is keenly aware of the limited time and the possibility that the judge will become frustrated with irrelevant or repetitive details. This is especially true with financial matters. The judge may listen to emotional tes-timony about the care of children, domestic violence or substance abuse. But when you are attempting to establish the righteousness of your money claims, facts and numbers are most important.

Once you have established that your spouse spent marital

funds on an extramarital sex partner, move on. If the lawyer
wastes too much time listing the same facts over and over again,
the judge may turn the disgust he feels for your spouse into anger
with you for wasting the court's time.

Don't give the opposing party an opportunity for rehabilita-
tion in the eyes of the court, no matter how eager you are to tell
the whole story. The time you spend on the witness stand answer-
ing questions from your attorney is when you establish your side
of the case. When the other side asks you questions, your ability
to respond is limited. Mostly, you are asked "yes or no" questions.

Most clients become frustrated when the lawyer on the other
side stops them, saying, "Please, just answer the question yes or
no." Sometimes the strategy of the other side is to purposely frus-
trate you, so you will lose your temper and show the judge what a
difficult person you are. An able family law specialist will prepare
you ahead of time by asking all those questions in the safety and
comfort of the law office. It's not necessarily what you say, but
how you say it, that makes a difference.

Get Witnesses to Court

One of the most distasteful aspects of a divorce trial is the
need to have friends and family members testify on your behalf.
While you can say all kinds of nice things about yourself, judges
— like most people — tend to believe others saying things about
you. You must be a good person if people will take the time and
risk alienating your spouse to make a point in your favor.

Sometimes these people are the only ones who can corrobo-
rate certain claims, such as whether you owned certain personal

property before your marriage. In complex property cases, you may call expert witnesses such as appraisers who can testify about the value of a home or business. Work with your attorney to decide who will testify for you and what questions they will be asked. Rely on the expertise of your attorney to figure out who will help you and who is extraneous to your case. As one judge says, "Even Adolph Hitler could get three people to say he is wonderful. That doesn't mean I would believe them."

Get Plenty of Rest

Nothing can bring on sleepless nights like a contested divorce case, especially when your financial well being is at issue. It is important that you come fully prepared, remembering what your attorney told you and what certain witnesses will say. It's also important that you come to court rested and ready for trial.

Try to take your mind off the proceedings the night before. Go to a movie or a sporting event. Don't succumb to pressure.

No matter what happens in court, your life will go on. And if you walk into court rested and refreshed, things always go better than you think they will.

Your Day in Court

From the moment you leave your home for the courthouse, you are part of the court system and should be careful how you look and act. For any court appearance, clients should dress professionally. For men, we recommend a suit or nice pair of slacks, a dress shirt and tie. A nice dress or suit is appropriate for a woman. If you have any questions about your wardrobe choices, be sure to ask your lawyer for suggestions. First impressions are important in all aspects of life, but they are crucial in a marital dispute where a judge is forced to evaluate the credibility of the parties in a short time.

If you are unable to settle your case, eventually it will be set for trial on the court's calendar. It is said that one-half of all cases filed in courts across the country involve some facet of family law. That's a lot of cases to demand time on the calendar. A case may be reset several times before it actually reaches trial. Continuances occur for a variety of reasons: the parties' readiness to try the case as well as conflicts in the attorneys' schedules; the client's schedule or the court's docket. If the judge is already in trial on another case or has an immediate issue to address or an older case to hear, your case may be passed over and continued to a later date.

A spouse who will owe money to the other spouse after the divorce often tries to continue the case as long as possible. This either avoids imposing a premature obligation on the client or forces a settlement in the case. Over time, many people become anxious to settle — even to the point of accepting an inadequate offer — because they've waited so long for their money.

Always appear calm and cool, even though deep down you may feel quite the opposite. Cases often settle because a client convinces the other side he or she is not concerned about going to trial.

Once you realize a settlement cannot be reached, it may be a long time before the case actually goes to trial. The delay needs to be factored into any decision surrounding settlement of the case and whether the expenses associated with the delay will be outweighed by the trial court's potential ruling.

Your spouse may not believe you will actually go to trial. In such cases, it is often beneficial for you to follow through with a trial. Otherwise, your spouse will continue to harass you after the divorce, believing he or she can get away with it.

Definitely Set For a Hearing, Maybe

For most people, a trip to the courthouse is an eye-opening experience. Because 10 to 15 cases may be set on the judge's docket the same day as your case, the parties and witnesses for each case on the docket fill the courtroom at the beginning of the day. The hallways outside the courtroom are often lined with hard wooden benches filled to capacity with more parties, witnesses and lawyers trying to resolve their cases at the last possible moment.

Usually, the judge calls the docket first thing in the morning and checks the status of each case with the attorneys representing the parties. The attorneys may request an opportunity to discuss settlement with each other. They may request a continuance or ask to speak with the judge about a particular issue that needs clarification before the case can proceed. If the parties are ready for trial, the judge will determine, based on all of the cases set that day, which one will be heard.

The judge's determination is based on a variety of factors.

First, the case with the oldest filing date usually has priority. Sometimes, the judge looks at the seriousness of the issues at hand. If there is an emergency issue on the docket — such as an immediate threat of abuse or theft of property — the court usually attempts to resolve this issue, even if it is only a short-term fix.

When several emergencies are set on the court's docket the same day as your case, the judge picks the most immediate emergency and one the court has time to handle. If the judge is already in trial on a case from the previous day, it is normal to proceed with that case and reschedule all the others. This is how the judicial system works, and your lawyer can't do much about it. Even though you probably waited months to get to trial, prepared for the trial with your lawyer and witnesses all present, your case may be continued.

Keep Your Cool in Court

During any court appearance, remain focused on the issue at hand. Sit up straight in your seat, speak clearly and be polite. Remember that the judge is evaluating your responses and your overall personality. Do not be argumentative or hostile with the other side or answer questions in a haughty or sarcastic fashion.

Your lawyer is the one to handle the relevant arguments, not you. The talented trial lawyer on the other side will want to get you upset on the stand so you will lose your temper and show the judge the evil personality that the other side has described. Human nature makes us all want to respond when attacked by another person. Keep in mind that the other side's goal is to affect your focus during the trial. Do not help them achieve their goal.

Tell the Truth Concisely

When the other side asks you questions, give truthful and accurate answers. Besides the fact that lying on the stand is unethical and illegal, it may ruin your credibility in front of the trial judge if the other side can discredit your testimony. Often you expect questions about factors that led to the breakup of the marriage. Discuss with your lawyer ahead of time how to handle these issues at trial. Do not offer more information than the other side has requested.

It is not your job to prove the other side's case. If the lawyer does not ask the appropriate questions, you may not have to provide certain information. This principle applies to every question you are asked. Once you have answered the question as briefly as possible, be quiet. If you have concerns about how to answer certain questions, you need to discuss these concerns with your lawyer beforehand.

Your lawyer will go over a specific plan for handling the case at trial, based on how he knows the judge in that particular court will respond to certain information. Even though you may think a fact or piece of evidence is absolutely imperative, it may annoy the judge and throw your lawyer off. Most divorce lawyers want to know exactly what you plan to say when you are on the stand. Your refusal to follow your lawyer's advice may cause you problems.

Wood ◆ Shaw

Details to Address

Whether your case was settled by agreement or tried by the judge, there will almost certainly be items to follow up on and tasks to complete to finalize various provisions of the Final Judgement of Divorce.

These items include the following:

- Prepare and file new real estate deeds
- Transfer title or bills of sale to automobiles, boats or other titled property
- Create and enter a Qualified Domestic Relations Order (QDRO) to divide a retirement account
- Prepare and file tax and insurance forms
- For women, file a name change with the correct governmental entity and with creditors
- Inform creditors of name or address changes
- Let friends and family members know the divorce is over, especially if you are looking for a job or other business opportunities

CHAPTER 23

Finalizing Details of the Divorce

O nce the divorce is complete and you have received your Final Judgement of Divorce, make sure you have a plan for handling the future. Many parties make a terrible mistake by continuing the bitterness they felt toward their spouse into the future. Once the divorce is over, make every effort to move forward.

It sounds like great advice. But in fact, moving forward is probably the most difficult challenge you will face. Many times, a client involved in the divorce process for a year or more resolves the divorce suddenly. At a moment's notice, you go from battle stations to your everyday life again. The first thing you should do after the divorce is rest and recover. Before making any major decisions, get off the emotional roller coaster you have been on during the divorce process.

What Does the Final Judgement of Divorce Say?

Once you have the Final Judgement of Divorce back from the court, make an appointment with your lawyer to go over the terms of the order. Make sure you understand them. Recognize that you may be charged with civil or criminal contempt of court if you intentionally violate or fail to follow the terms of the order. Make certain you understand your obligations and your spouse's obligations under the decree. After taking a little time, you may be in a better frame of mind to absorb and understand all the intricacies of the agreement and any requirements imposed on you by the document. Read the Final Judgement of Divorce several times and make a list of questions to ask your lawyer. If your case was tried and you received an order written by the judge, you may need clarification on the terms of the order. You may be able to handle this meeting by telephone, but it may require a lengthy meeting to go over all the terms and requirements.

The settlement agreement or Final Judgement of Divorce may outline the timing, means and method for completing many of tasks. But sometimes the document is silent about these matters. Third parties such as banks, mortgage companies, insurance companies, title companies or retirement plan administrators — because of their practices and procedures — cause delays in the implementation of orders. Your former spouse, of course, can also drag his or her feet or refuse to reasonably act or respond to your efforts to move forward.

It may be necessary to file a motion with the trial court to require your former spouse to sign a deed, provide health insurance cards or take other steps to complete the divorce process. Dealing with these post-divorce details can be frustrating and entail tremendous time and effort. It can be expensive if you pay your lawyer to deal with such matters. Many, if not all, of these details can be handled by you if you can stand the hassle.

Discuss these issues with your attorney and have a clear understanding of what tasks you expect your attorney to complete and how much it will cost. Appendix 14 is a post-divorce checklist of items that often need to be addressed to effectuate the provisions of the Final Judgement of Divorce and complete the divorce process. We strongly recommend that you review this list after you have received your divorce decree, to help insure that the necessary steps are taken to finalize and complete your divorce.

Your Annual Divorce Tuneup

Complex settlement agreements have a way of changing over time. Businesses grow or go bust. Real property is sold. Taxes are paid or, worse, left unpaid. Your view of yourself and the experience of divorce changes with the passing of time.

An increasingly popular idea is an annual divorce tuneup. It's a simple process that begins with a rereading of your settlement agreement or Final Judgement of Divorce and any additional motions or modifications. Prepare a list of questions and make an appointment with your attorney, accountant or financial planner. Talk to the professional who communicates best with you, getting answers to questions that may have arisen in the past year. Your attorney can be especially helpful, updating you on any changes in the law since your divorce.

An appeal is a last-ditch effort to overturn a court order and often will fail. The standard of review for an appeal is stringent. Most deal with specific issues like whether certain evidence or testimony should have been allowed.

CHAPTER 24

One More Bite at the Apple

Y ou've had your day in court. This was your one big attempt to show that you deserve to run the family business or should receive periodic alimony. In most cases, this is your one time in a courtroom. Overturning the trial court's decision in a divorce case is difficult and rare. That's why it is so important to prepare your case well and get what you need either through settlement or trial. Still, there are two main avenues available for post-judgment review and relief — a motion for a new trial and an appeal to a higher court.

Motion to Set Aside or for a New Trial

Either party may file a motion to set aside the decree or request a new trial if you are not satisfied with the court's ruling.

Under Alabama law, this type of motion generally must be filed within 30 days of the date of your Final Judgement of Divorce.

In reality, a motion like this usually is not successful unless the court failed to consider a material fact in evidence or the court made a clear and distinct error in its ruling. The trial judge heard your entire case. He is familiar with it and can review his notes to determine if an error occurred. With a motion for a new trial, you are asking the trial judge to admit that he or she made a mistake and needs to correct it. If this type of motion is not successful, you are then forced to use the appeals process to change things.

Last-Ditch Effort

An appeal is a difficult legal procedure that can cost far more than the divorce itself. You have 42 days after the Final Judgement of Divorce is issued to appeal to a higher court. The lawyer begins by writing a history of the case. If you hire a different lawyer to handle the appeal, he or she will spend many hours getting familiar with the case before writing the appeal. If the appeal is not successful and the matter is then appealed to the state Supreme Court, the lawyer may have to draft additional documents.

So you see, it is much more effective and efficient to handle the case properly at trial. Relying on the appeals process to remedy an injustice that occurred at trial is possible, but it's a long shot.

Modifications

The details of most divorces are completed within a few months after the Final Judgement of Divorce is signed by the

judge. Others linger because of motions for a new trial or ap.
A few go on for years, due to efforts to modify the divorce decree

The most common modifications involve the support and care of children. No party to a divorce should say at the outset that what happens in the original divorce action isn't important just because a modification can be obtained. Modifications are expensive and disruptive to the lives of everyone involved. You should think long and hard about the effect of any return to the court system. Is this action entirely necessary? Are there other ways to accomplish what you want? And will the positive effect of the modification offset the negative effect of bringing the action?

The requirement for almost any modification is that a "material change of circumstance" has taken place since the last court hearing. This means there is a basic change in the lives of the parents or the children. This makes a modification of the terms of the divorce possible based on the legal standard applied to the particular type of modification.

More or Less Child Support

A financial windfall for either party to a divorce should benefit the children just as it would if the family had remained intact. Kids get new bicycles and larger rooms in fancier houses when the parents make more money. Increases or decreases in the income of either party influence modifications to prior child support awards.

If the payor spouse's income has increased significantly, the recipient parent may be entitled to more child support. If the payor spouse has lost a job or decreased his or her income significantly, the amount of child support may be reduced. Periodic changes in the child support guidelines may be reason enough for payments to change.

Both parents have a duty to support their children the best they can. If the parent making child support payments pays for expenses and activities over and above the mandated child support obligation, you must take that into consideration. You may not want to risk having those extra payments discontinued by fighting for a slight increase in child support. Most matrimonial law experts can calculate the projected new child support payment under your facts, provided you have the gross monthly income figures for both parents as well as any day care and health insurance expenses.

Nowhere in divorce do the emotional and the financial collide like they do in child support. Sometimes an attempt to get more support can turn from strictly financial to a custody battle. This action may be apparent to the court as an effort to avoid paying higher child support, but it can create considerable problems and expense for the custodial parent who is seeking the increase.

If you have had less than exemplary conduct since the divorce, you may not want to ask for a modification of child support because custody could come into question. The fact that you, as a custodial parent, are living with a friend of the opposite sex may not seem like a big deal to you. But it can cloud the issue of child support and lead to a counter-petition by the other parent for custody of the children.

For every action in family court, there is an equal and opposite reaction. Modifications give rise to many reactions that people may have never considered in advance.

Issues in Reserve

Some issues in a divorce may be considered too early to decide, so they are kept in reserve until a later date. A perfect example is post-majority college support. If your child is three years old when the divorce takes place, it is virtually impossible to predict if he or she will go to college or how much college will cost when the children is ready to go.

This issue may be held in reserve until the child is in high school. At that time, you may petition the court to compel your spouse to pay college expenses if you can't reach an agreement on them.

"You have to be willing to change the way you think, feel and act in relationship to yourself and others. It can be difficult. But this is wiping the slate clean, hitting the erase button and starting over."

Counselor Elise Smith Chatham

CHAPTER 25

Moving On

Once your divorce is final, everyone around you may assume that all your problems are over. However, your divorce may be just one chapter in a lengthy book with many other chapters left to explore.

It has been said that you don't go to divorce court for justice. You simply go for a conclusion. It is impossible to bring fairness into an emotionally destructive process such as a divorce in a manner that will make everyone happy. Many times a person will spend years being extremely angry with a former spouse and bitter over facts that cannot be changed. While a certain amount of emotion and anger is justified, don't ruin the rest of your life worrying about the behavior of others. We frequently tell clients that when God closes a door, he often opens a window. We recommend that clients look for that window rather than spending time banging their heads against a closed door.

Saving Your Assets

One former client, Sharon, a divorced mother of one daughter, offers the following insight on moving forward after a painful divorce.

> *When my husband left me for another woman, I was devastated and humiliated. I had remained faithful and devoted to him throughout our marriage. It was shocking to discover the man I trusted completely had deceived me. I decided to build a new life for my daughter and me, without him. I decided to be better, not bitter. Looking back, I believe there were three things that helped me move forward: God, the support of family and friends and a positive attitude.*
>
> *I relied on God every day to guide me through the enormous stress of divorce settlement, to lift me out of depression, to overcome anger, to help me find a job and to find the words to console my daughter as she grieved for the loss of family life.*
>
> *I sought comfort from my parents, other family members and close friends. I spent countless hours talking out my problems to keep my sanity and ran up huge phone bills that were worth every penny. I was also quick to call my divorce attorney's legal assistant whenever I needed advice or just to talk to someone who understood. She was a great counselor and friend who was always there for me.*
>
> *Finally, having a positive outlook on life was essential. I have hope for the future that my life will*

once again be happy and full. But this journey hasn't been easy. There is a trail of emotional garbage left behind to clean up, especially when a child is involved. So, I take it a day at a time. I am beginning to see the light at the end of the tunnel. I will succeed at reinventing my life.

Ken, a sales trainer and motivational speaker, had a difficult task. While working in a high-energy environment, he grieved for the loss of his childhood sweetheart.

I thought we had the ideal life – two wonderful kids, exciting jobs, a nice home and plenty of friends. Then one day she told me, out of the blue, that she couldn't do this anymore. This was not how she saw her life unfolding. She wanted out, and she did just that. She disappeared with only her clothes and her car. Our children didn't know where she was, and neither did I. She could have been kidnapped, but I knew she wasn't.

For months I had to get up in front of training sessions or give speeches that inspired salespeople to do their best. I could barely stand there without breaking into tears. My heart was breaking, but I had to put on a show. I couldn't grieve in private. I could only put on a mask and pretend that everything was fine.

A year passed before she surfaced again. It was obvious that she needed money and so she came back into our lives. She didn't want the responsibilities of being a wife and mother, but she wanted the benefits. She had taken nothing with her when she left, and now she wanted her part. So about the time I was getting my head on straight, I had to deal with the anger and frustration of a divorce.

I let her know that if she would fulfill her role as a mother, I would give in to many of her demands. It all went surprisingly well. Several years have passed since this happened. I've gotten over her terrible behavior because she is a very good mother. It's the most I could have expected from the situation, and it's what I have gotten.

Advice from a Counselor

Counselor Elise Smith Chatham says major life changes usually happen one step at a time. "You have to be willing to change your position on some deep beliefs, emotions, and behavioral patterns," she says. "Until you begin to live with dignity, respect and emotional integrity, you will not have that quality and level of interaction with anyone else. To quote Dr. Phil McGraw, 'You must decide that you are willing to let yourself want and reach and dream. Set goals, make a strategy and take action.' Life is managed, it is not cured. Learn to take charge of your life."

Nancy Wasson, Ph.D., says that according to one source, half of women and one-third of men are still intensely angry at their former spouse years after the divorce. "What a heavy suitcase to carry around 10 years later, not to mention the increased health risks and on-going mental agitation," Wasson says. "Since everything in our lives requires energy, when we remain connected to past events we have less energy available for use in the present moment. Hanging on to anger, hatred, resentment and bitterness only hurts our children and us. When we are able to process our feelings, release the pain and forgive ourselves and our ex-spouse, then we are in the best possible place to construct a new life that has peace, depth and quality."

Identity Restructuring after A Divorce

Psychologist Bonnie Atkinson offers the following ideas on rebuilding your identity after a divorce:

> The best approach is to look at divorce as one would look at any loss; it is an identity restructuring. When a child dies, you do not now feel like a mother. When a parent dies, you no longer feel parented. When you lose a spouse through divorce, you are no longer living the life of a married person. Literally, the task is to relearn how to be in the world of relationships. These are identity issues because you usually define yourself in relationships. For instance, you may be a neighbor, a church member, a member of a nonprofit board, a participant on a team or a member of the psychology association. When the marital relationship changes it is necessary to choose how you will be now in relation to all these people and groups. Just as grieving is not a process of pas-

sively moving through prescribed stages, but a developmental task to relearn, so too is divorce recovery a process of learning. You must relearn holiday rituals, vacations, meal plans, budgeting, yard work and friends. That is, you have the job of changing relationships with others, those with the children, the ex-spouse and friends. It has all changed and you must work to make relationships fit with this new role as a single person; these are identity issues.

You feel differently in the world as a single person. It is easy to feel that society functions like Noah's Ark, two-by-two. Taking the time to create a new life means having changed relationships, making new relationships and developing a new sense of self. It is an opportunity for making your life much richer and fuller. This is more than just an emotional coming back or getting through the pain of disappointment or despair. The task is not to simply "get back to normal" after the discord and chaos of the divorce process, but to give yourself time to change old beliefs and habits into new ways that work better. If one always drove 500 miles with the family to share Thanksgiving with the in-laws or parents for the holiday, what happens after the divorce? Will the children be with you? Now that you have to go back to work, can you get time off to go away with family? Have you ever driven 500 miles alone? Are you welcome there this year? Are you vested in doing the big turkey day ritual of cooking?

There is much to relearn; recovery after a divorce is a process of healing and changing your sense of self to have a new identity. The lifelong process of adult development is thrown into crisis by the sudden change of divorce, but the identity work is important for real happiness.

"Divorce gave me the opportunity to do things I had never been able to do in my marriage. The advice I received allowed me to be financially protected and emotionally secure."

A Former Client

CHAPTER 26

Parting Words of Wisdom

If you forget everything else from this book, remember this; your divorce could be the most important legal and financial matter you will go through in your life. Don't blow it through inattention or the need for revenge. Make every effort to handle your divorce as wisely as possible. Attempt to address in the settlement agreement every possible issue that might arise after the divorce.

How you handle your divorce will greatly impact potential problems you will have to deal with in the future. If you do not realize how much the divorce will impact your future, talk to people who have been divorced for several years. There is usually an immediate financial impact on each party as a result of the divorce. Proceed with knowledge and a sound plan for handling the issues you will face both during and after the divorce.

Saving Your Assets

Consult with an expert familiar with matrimonial law in your area before proceeding with any action in a divorce. Do not execute any documents without the advice and approval of your attorney. Your spouse's attorney cannot advise you as to the consequences of your actions and you should not rely on his or her advice. If a divorce is going to happen whether you want it or not, prepare to deal with the potential outcome. It is similar to finding out that you have cancer. Obviously, you did not want the cancer, but it is imperative that you get expert medical advice concerning your treatment. Divorce is similar to the cancer example. If you put your head in the sand and try to ignore it, it will only get worse. Once you have retained counsel, you should consult with your attorney about the actions needed to protect yourself and your children.

Take a proactive approach from the beginning. Get the financial records you need to prove the amount of assets and liabilities at stake in the divorce. Assert your rights in the matter of child support, alimony and temporary maintenance. And understand that fault plays a part in the division of property and all other issues in the divorce.

Once you have obtained the divorce, move forward. Do not ruin the rest of your life worrying about whether you could have done things differently.

If you can achieve this type of result, you will truly have achieved the successful financial divorce.

Good luck.

References

1. From a telephone survey of 1,278 adult Americans taken for TIME/CNN on September 6-7, 2000 by Yankelovich Partners, Inc.

2. Bureau of Vital Statistics.

3. Yanlelovich Partners, Inc. for TIME/CNN.

4. Mary Wier, CDP, is the owner of Horizons Planning, a personal financial consulting firm specializing in divorce issues. Advisory Services offered through Investment Advisors, a division of ProEquities, Inc., a Registered Investment Adviser and a Registered Broker/ Dealer, member NASD & SIPC. Horizons Planning is independent of ProEquities, Inc. Miss Wier can be reached at (205) 871-7743 or www.horizonsfinancial.com.

5. Yip, Pamela. Personal Finance column. Business section, The Dallas Morning News (July 23, 2001), 1H.

6. Kristof, Kathy. Personal Finance column, Business (Los Angeles Times Syndicate, October 26, 1997).

7. Ibid.

8. The National Marriage Project (Rutgers University, 2000): 26.

9. Lake, Steven R. and Feldman, Ruth Diskin. Rematch (Chicago: Chicago Review Press, 1989).

10. Lake and Feldman.

11. The National Marriage Project.

Saving Your Assets

Appendices of Exhibits

NOTE: Appendices 1-7 are lists of professionals with experience helping Alabama residents through divorce. Neither the authors nor the publisher guarantee the services of these providers. There are many other experienced professionals in the state not on our lists. These lists are merely a resource for divorcing people attempting to solve problems unique to their situation.

Appendix 1
Alabama Accountants

David Barker, CPA
Dewitt & Dyer, L.L.C.
521 Energy Center Blvd., Suite 1501, Northport, AL 35472
Telephone: (205) 345-9898 or 888-345-0335

Pam Clark, C.P.A
Donaldson, Holman & West, P.C
3595 Grandview Parkway, Suite 100, Birmingham, AL 35243
Telephone (205) 278-0001

Kenneth C. Dewitt, C.P.A., C.F.A.
Dewitt & Dyer, L.L.C.
521 Energy Center Blvd., Suite 1501, Northport, AL 35472
Telephone: (205) 345-9898 or 888-345-0335

Anthony J. DiPiazza, C.P.A.
DiPiazza, Larocca, McDowell, and Cade
600 Luckie Drive, Suite 300, Birmingham, AL 35223
Telephone (205) 871-9973

Tim Downard, C.P.A
Haynes, Downard, Andra, and Jones, LLP
2 North 20th Street, Suite 550, Birmingham, AL 35203
Telephone (205) 254-3380

Raiford G. "Ray" Dyer, Jr., C.P.A., M.T.A.
Dewitt & Dyer, L.L.C.
521 Energy Center Blvd., Suite 1501, Northport, AL 35472
Telephone: (205) 345-9898 or 888-345-0335

Paul B. Fields, Jr., C.P.A.
Wilson, Price, Barranco, Blakenship & Billingsly, P.C.
3815 Interstate Court, Montgomery, AL 36109
Telephone: (334) 271-2200

Bryan Finison, M.B.A., A.V.A.
Dewitt & Dyer, L.L.C.
521 Energy Center Blvd., Suite 1501, Northport, AL 35472
Telephone: (205) 345-9898 or 888-345-0335

G. Alan Hartley, C.P.A.
Morrison& Smith, L.L.P.
1809 University Blvd.
Tuscaloosa, AL 35401

George A. Henry, III, C.P.A., C.V.A.
Henry & Alm, P.C.
120 Southside Square
Huntsville, AL 35801
Telephone: (256) 539-9641

Mike Jackson, C.P.A
Jackson, Howard, and Whatley
729 Chestnut Street, Birmingham, AL 35216
Telephone (205) 822-2352

William D. Smith, C.P.A.
Morrison& Smith, L.L.P.
1809 University Blvd.
Tuscaloosa, Alabama 35401

John West, C.P.A
Donaldson, Holman & West, P.C
3595 Grandview Parkway, Suite 100, Birmingham, AL 35243
Telephone (205) 278-0001

Randy Whirley, C.P.A
Whirley and Associates
1 Perimeter Park South, Suite 100 North, Birmingham, AL 35243
Telephone (205) 970-6034

Appendix 2
Alabama Financial Planners

Birmingham

Stewart Welch, III
The Welch Group
3940 Montclair Road, 5th Floor, Birmingham, AL 35213
Telephone: (205) 879-5001

James W. Baxter
3500 Colonnade Parkway, Suite 150, Birmingham, AL 35243
Telephone: (205) 970-5200

Greg Canfield
The Canfield Agency
701 Montgomery Highway, Vestavia Hills, AL 35216
Telephone: (205) 822-5477

Steven Gill
3500 Colonnade Parkway,
Birmingham, AL 35243
Telephone: (205) 970-5286

Saving Your Assets

Charles D. Haines
Charles D. Haines, L.L.C.
600 University Place, Suite 501, Birmingham, AL 35209
Telephone: (205) 871-3334

Brandy Hydrick, C.F.A.
Charles D. Haines, L.L.C.
600 University Place, Suite 501, Birmingham, AL 35209
Telephone: (205) 871-3334

Robert Ireland
Merrill Lynch
420 North 20th Street, Birmingham, AL 35203
Telephone: (205) 326-9543

Robert R. Lott, C.L.U., C.H.F.C.
3500 Colonnade Parkway, Suite 130, Birmingham, AL 35242
Telephone: (205) 380-2600

Sherry Robinson, C.P.A, C.F.P.
Charles D. Haines, L.L.C.
600 University Place, Suite 501, Birmingham, AL 35209
Telephone: (205) 871-3334

Dawn Peeples, Financial Representative
2900 Highway 280, Suite 210, Birmingham, AL 35223
Telephone: (205) 271-7016

Stewart Webb, Financial Consultant
Smith Barney
3500 Colonnade Parkway, Suite 200, Birmingham, AL 35243
Telephone: (205) 969-7055

Mary Wier, Certified Divorce Planner
Horizons Planning
3900 Montclair Rd., Birmingham, AL 35213
Telephone: (205) 871- 7743

Pete J. Wright, C.L.U.
Financial Principles & Concepts, L.L.C.
2000 Southbridge Parkway, Birmingham, AL 35209
Telephone: (205) 871-9993

Florence

Michael R. Jones
P.O. Drawer 2107, Decatur, AL 35602
Telephone: (256) 353-8224

Karen King
603 E Second Street, Sheffield, AL 35660
Telephone: (256) 383-6711

Huntsville

Randy Bennett
1200 Winner Avenue SW, Huntsville, AL 35805
Telephone: (256) 536-9580

Mobile

Patrick Dunn, C.L.U.
One Office Park, Suite 307
P.O. Box 91627, Mobile, AL 36691
Telephone: (334) 344 -1480

Gaynell Palmisano
1420 Government Street
Mobile, Alabama 36604
Telephone: (251) 476-8011

Duane W. Tressler
Three Office Park, Suite 110
Mobile, Alabama 36609
Telephone: (334) 343-4855

Appendix 3
Alabama Estate Planners

Charles Barton Adcox
Phelps, Jenkins, Gibson & Fowler, L.L.P.
P.O. Box 020848, Tuscaloosa, AL 35402-0848
Telephone: (205) 345-5100

William J. Bryant
Feld, Hyde, Lyle, Wertheimer & Bryant, P.C
Suite 500, 2000 Southbridge Parkway, Birmingham, AL 35209
Telephone (205) 802-7575

John J. Crowley, Jr.
Coale, Dukes, Kirkpatrick & Crowley
2610 B Dauphin Street, Suite 101, Mobile, AL 36606-4802
Telephone: (334) 471-2625

C. Fred Daniels
Cabiness, Johnston, Gardner, Dumas & O'Neal
2001 Park Place North, Birmingham, AL 35203
Telephone: (205) 716-5232

Richard Mark Kirkpatrick
Coale, Dukes, Kirkpatrick & Crowley
2610 B Dauphin Street, Suite 101, Mobile, AL 36606-4802
Telephone: (334) 471-2625

Melinda Matthews
Sirote & Permutt
2311 Highland Avenue South, Suite 500, Birmingham, AL 35205
Telephone: (205) 930-5101

Appendix 4
Alabama Psychologists/Psychiatrists/Counselors/Therapists

Birmingham

Alabama Psychotherapy & Wellness Center, P.C.
631 Beacon Parkway West, Suite 203, Birmingham, AL 35209
Telephone: (205) 912-2000

Dr. Karen Turnbow
Alabama Psychotherapy & Wellness Center, P.C.
631 Beacon Parkway West, Suite 203, Birmingham, AL 35209
Telephone: (205) 912-2000

Dr. Sharon Gotlieb
Alabama Psychotherapy & Wellness Center, P.C.
631 Beacon Parkway West, Suite 203, Birmingham, AL 35209
Telephone: (205) 912-2000

Dr. Travis Tindal
Covenant House
3001 Cahaba Heights Road, Birmingham, AL 35243
Telephone: (205) 967-3575

Nancy J. Wasson
Fox Run Counseling Services
3411 Caseys Crossing, Birmingham, AL 35215
Telephone: (205) 680-4311

Elise Smith Chatham, L.C.S.W.
Family and Life Consultant
350 Canyon Park Drive, Pelham, AL 35214
Telephone: (205) 807-8118

Fletcher Hamilton, Ph.D.
One Independence Plaza, Birmingham, AL 35209
Telephone: (205) 871-0031

Paul G. LaRussa, M.D.
350 Canyon Park Drive, Pelham, AL 35214
Telephone: (205) 664-8721

Kyle Echols, M.D.
1903 Oxmoor Road, Homewood, AL 35209
Telephone: (205) 879-2700

Denise L. Fournet, Ph.D
Licensed Clinical Psychologist
1903 Oxmoor Road, Homewood, AL 35209
Telephone: (205) 879-2700

Beth Jacobs, Ph.D.
Licensed Clinical Psychologist
1903 Oxmoor Road, Homewood, AL 35209
Telephone: (205) 879-2700

Grayson & Associates, P.C.
Gayle Pelham, Ph.D.
Robert M. Pitts, Jr., Psy.D.
Steven Kaczor, Psy.D., J.D.
10 Old Montgomery Highway, Suite 100, Homewood, AL 35209
Telephone: (205) 871-6926

New Life Clinic
Kelly Cousins, L.P.C.
Melinda Higginbotham
Dr. Laura English
Arlee Arban
200 Office Park Drive, Birmingham, AL 35223
Telephone: (205) 879-9964

Adult & Child Development Professionals
Cotton, McInturff, Wade & Associates, P.C.
James P. Cotton, M.Ed., M.F.T.
Robbin C. McInturff, M.A., M.F.T.
Kenneth I. Wade, Ph.D, M.F.T.
Rebecca I. Dossett, Ph.D., M.F.T.
Marian B. Elledge, M.A.
Glenda R. Elliott, Ph.D.
Beebe E. Roberts, M.A., M.F.T.
Keith D. Thompson, M.A.
2305 Arlington Avenue, Birmingham, AL 35205
Telephone: (205) 933- 9276

Family Therapy Associates
Bob Wendorf, Psy.D., L.M.S.P.
Don Wendorf, Psy.D., L.M.S.P.
Harriet Schaeffer, M.A., L.M.S.P.
Sharon Turner, Ph.D.
813 Shades Creek Parkway, Homewood, AL 35209
Telephone: (205) 870-5955

Huntsville

Alabama Psychiatric Services
Adult & Adolescent Counseling
7618 Memorial Parkway South, Huntsville, AL 35802
Telephone: (256) 882-7703

Clinton Clay, L.C.S.W.
3322 Century Office Center, Huntsville, AL 35810
Telephone: (256) 881-0884

Luther E. Kramer, L.P.C.
North Alabama Center for Pastoral Counseling
219 Grove Avenue, Huntsville, AL 35801
Telephone: (256) 534-2560

Dr. Stephen Taylor
Child Psychiatrist
Alabama Psychiatric Services
7618 Memorial Parkway South, Huntsville, AL 35802
Telephone: (256) 882-7703

Family Services Center, Inc.
2227 Drake Avenue S.W., Huntsville, AL 35805
Telephone: (256) 551-1610

Zane Slocumb, L.P.C., N.C.C., D.A.P.A.
7618 South Memorial Parkway, Huntsville, AL 35802
Telephone: (256) 882-7703

Florence/Muscle Shoals/Tuscumbia

Dr. Bonnie L. Atkinson, Ph.D.
444 North Cedar Street, Florence, AL
Telephone: (256) 767-6139

Mobile

Alice H. Frederick, Ph.D.
131 Fairhope Avenue, Fairhope, AL 36532
Telephone: (205) 928-5656

Crossway Counseling Center
27625 U.S. Highway 98, Bldg. A, Dephne, AL 336526
Telephone: 9334) 626-2959

Montgomery

Sharon Bell, L.P.C.
Licensed Marriage & Family Therapist
505 South Perry Street, Montgomery, AL 36104
Telephone: (334) 265-1009

Karl Kirkland, Ph.D.
Kirkland, King & Renfro
1520 Mulberry Street, Montgomery, AL 36106
Telephone: (334) 269-1106

Guy Renfro, Ph.D
Kirkland, King & Renfro
1520 Mulberry Street, Montgomery, AL 36106
Telephone: (334) 269-1106

Glen King, J.D., Ph.D.
Kirkland, King & Renfro
1520 Mulberry Street, Montgomery, AL 36106
Telephone: (334) 269-1106

Appendix 5
Alabama Church/Pastoral Counselors

Birmingham

Samaritan Counseling Center of Baptist Health Systems
3900 Montclair Road, Birmingham, AL 35213
(205) 870-5190

Bart Grooms, Pastoral Counselor
Samaritan Counseling Center
1114 Oxmoor Road, Birmingham, AL 35209
Telephone: (205) 871-7324

Daphne T. Dickinson, L.P.C.
Alabama Counseling Institute
3928 Montclair Road, Suite 100, Birmingham, AL 35213
Telephone: (205) 871-1713

Dr. Dixon Mitchell
Cantebury Counseling Center
350 Overbrook Road, Mountain Brook, AL 35213
Telephone: (205) 879-0202

Covenant Counseling & Education Center
2204 Lakeshore Drive, Suite 214, Birmingham, AL 35209
Telephone:(205) 879-7500

Alabama Baptist Children's Counseling Center
P.O. Box 19792, Birmingham, AL 35219

Briarwood Presbyterian Church Counseling Center
Attention: Counseling
2200 Briarwood Way, Birmingham, AL 35243
Telephone: (205) 978-2200

The Church at Brook Hills
Attention: Counseling
3145 Brook Highland Parkway, Birmingham, AL
Telephone: (205) 991-0507

Huntsville

Amanda W. Ragland
Vine Pastoral Counseling Center
Telephone: (256) 461-8580

Crisis Service Center of North Alabama
Luther E. Kramer, L.P.C.
219 Grove Avenue, Huntsville, AL 35801
Telephone: (256) 534-2560

Whitesburg Baptist Church
Attention: Counseling
6806 Whitesburg Drive South, Huntsville, AL
Telephone: (256) 881-0952

Anniston

Allen D. Lindell
Grays Pastoral Counseling Center
Telephone: (256) 236-1496

Decatur/Florence/Muscle Shoals/Tuscumbia

New Life Christian Church
Attention: Counseling
1200 Welti Road SE, Cullman, AL
Telephone: (256) 734-4816

Mobile

Daphne United Methodist Church
Attention: Counseling
2401 Main Street, Daphne, AL
Telephone: (251) 626-2287

Montgomery

First Baptist Church
305 S. Perry Street, Montgomery, AL
Telephone: (334) 834-6310

Tuscaloosa

First Wesleyan Church
Attention: Counseling
1501 McFarland Blvd. North, Tuscaloosa, AL
Telephone: (205) 752-4251

First Baptist Church
Attention: Counseling
721 Greensboro Avenue, Tuscaloosa, AL
Telephone: (205) 345-7554

Appendix 6
Alabama Mortgage Companies

Coats & Company
Rob Coats, President
2000-B Southbridge Parkway, Suite 150, Birmingham, AL 35209
Telephone: (205) 871-5600

Diversified Mortgage
Regina D. Clement, Manager
3512 Old Montgomery Highway, Birmingham, AL 35209
Telephone: (205) 871-5626

Magellan Mortgage Services, Inc.
Clay Wilkinson, President
2004 G Poole Drive, Huntsville, AL 35810
Telephone: (256) 859-9696

First Commercial Bank
Chris Robbins, Assistant Vice President
800 Shades Creek Parkway, Birmingham, AL 35209
Telephone: (205) 868-4744

New South Federal Savings Bank
Randy Brown, Vice President
1900 Crestwood Boulevard, Birmingham, AL 35210
Telephone: (205) 951-7164

Online Payment and Mortgage Calculator
www.magellanmortgage.com

Appendix 7
Alabama Divorce Recovery Groups

Opelika/Auburn

Auburn United Methodist Church
137 South Gay Street, Auburn, AL
Telephone: (334) 826-8800

First Assembly of God
3777 Highway 431 N., Phoenix City, AL
Telephone: (334) 298-9890

Birmingham

Dawson Memorial Baptist Church
1114 Oxmoor Road, Birmingham, AL 35209
Telephone (205) 871-7324

Our Lady of Sorrows
1720 Oxmoor Road, Birmingham, AL 35209
Telephone (205) 871-8121

Briarwood Presbyterian Church Counseling Center
2200 Briarwood Way, Birmingham, AL 35243
Telephone: (205) 978-2200

Hunter Street Baptist Church
2600 John Hawkins Pike, Hoover, AL 35244
Telephone: (205) 985-7295

The Church at Brook Hills
3145 Brook Highland Parkway, Birmingham, AL
Telephone: (205) 991-0507

Valleydale Baptist Church
2545 Valleydale Road, Birmingham, AL
Telephone: (205) 991-5282

Dothan

Calvary Baptist Church
901 Montezuma Avenue,Dothan, AL
Telephone: (334) 792-5159

First Baptist Church
300 W. Main Street, Dothan, Alabama
Telephone: (334) 792-5117

New Freedom Church
115 Depot Street, Webb, Alabama
Telephone: (334) 702-8234

Fort Rucker Counseling
Building 8945 7th Avenue, Fort Rucker, Alabama
Telephone: (334) 255-3692

Decatur/Florence/Muscle Shoals/Tuscumbia

New Life Christian Church
1200 Welti Road SE, Cullman, Alabama
Telephone: (256) 734-4816

Calvary Assembly of God
1413 Glenn Street, SW, Decatur, Alabama
Telephone: (256) 355-7440

Decatur Baptist Church
2527 Danville Road, Decatur, Alabama
Telephone: (256) 353-8579

Huntsville

Whitesburg Baptist Church
6806 Whitesburg Drive South, Huntsville, Alabama
Telephone: (256) 881-0952

Pulaski Pike Church of God
3912 Pulaski Pike, Huntsville, Alabama
Telephone: (256) 852-5580

Willowbrook Baptist Church
7625 Bailey Cove Road, Huntsville, Alabama
Telephone: (256) 883-5433

First Church of the Nazarene
800 East Clinton Avenue, Huntsville, Alabama
Telephone: (256) 534-5364

Mobile

Daphne United Methodist Church
2401 Main Street, Daphne, Alabama
Telephone: (251) 626-2287

First Baptist Church North Mobile
1251 Industrial Parkway, Saraland, Alabama
Telephone: (334) 679-3266

Cottage Hill Baptist Church
4255 Cottage Hill Road, Mobile, Alabama
Telephone: (334) 660-2422

Forest Hill Church of God
5508 Moffett Road, Mobile, Alabama
Telephone: (334) 342-0233

First Baptist Church
15898 Silverhill Avenue, Silverhill, Alabama
Telephone: (334) 945-5182

Dauphin Way Baptist Church
3661 Dolphin St., Mobile, Alabama
Telephone: (334) 342-3456

Christ United Methodist Church
6101 Grelot Road, Mobile, Alabama
Telephone: (334) 342-0462

Foley United Methodist Church
915 N. Pine Street, Foley, Alabama
Telephone: (334) 943-4393

Montgomery

First Baptist Church
305 S. Perry Street, Montgomery, Alabama
Telephone: (334) 834-6310

Heritage Baptist Church
1849 Perry Hill Road, Montgomery, Alabama
Telephone: (334) 279-7176

Frazer Memorial United Methodist
6000 Atlanta Highway, Montgomery, Alabama
Telephone: (334) 260-3654

First Baptist Church
210 Sixth Street North. Clanton, AL
Telephone: (205) 755-3840

Faith Temple Church of God
4520 46th Street SW, Lanett, Alabama
Telephone: (334) 576-3904

Eastern Hills Baptist Church
3604 Pleasant Ridge Road, Montgomery, Alabama
Telephone: (334) 272-0604

First United Methodist Church
2416 W. Cloverdale Park, Montgomery, Alabama
Telephone: (334) 834-8990

First United Methodist Church
3350 Edgewood Drive, Millbrook, Alabama
Telephone: (334) 285-4114

Tuscaloosa

Valley View Baptist Church
8820 Highway 69 South, Tuscaloosa, Alabama
Telephone: (205) 752-0977

First Wesleyan Church
1501 McFarland Blvd. North, Tuscaloosa, Alabama
Telephone: (205) 752-4251

First Baptist Church
721 Greensboro Avenue, Tuscaloosa, Alabama
Telephone: (205) 345-7554

Appendix 8
House Net Equity Form

Current Estimated Market Value	$
Less 1st Mortgage on Property	$
Less Equity Line or 2nd Mortgage	$
Less Real Estate Commission	$
Less Closing Costs	$
ESTIMATED NET EQUITY IN RESIDENCE	$

Appendix 9
IRS Tax Exemption Form 8332

Form **8332**	**Release of Claim to Exemption**	OMB No. 1545-0915
(Rev. December 2000)	**for Child of Divorced or Separated Parents**	
Department of the Treasury Internal Revenue Service	▶ **Attach** to noncustodial parent's return **each year** exemption is claimed. **Caution:** *Do not use this form if you were never married.*	Attachment Sequence No. **115**

Name of noncustodial parent claiming exemption	Noncustodial parent's social security number (SSN) ▶	⋮ ⋮

Part I   **Release of Claim to Exemption for Current Year**

I agree not to claim an exemption for_____
Name(s) of child (or children)

for the tax year 20_____ .

Signature of custodial parent releasing claim to exemption	Custodial parent's SSN	Date

Note: *If you choose not to claim an exemption for this child (or children) for future tax years, also complete Part II.*

Part II   **Release of Claim to Exemption for Future Years** (If completed, see **Noncustodial parent** below.)

I agree not to claim an exemption for_____
Name(s) of child (or children)

for the tax year(s)_____
(Specify. See instructions.)

Signature of custodial parent releasing claim to exemption	Custodial parent's SSN	Date

General Instructions

Purpose of form. If you are a **custodial parent** and you were ever married to the child's **noncustodial parent**, you may use this form to release your claim to your child's exemption. To do so, complete this form (or a similar statement containing the same information required by this form) and give it to the noncustodial parent who will claim the child's exemption. The noncustodial parent must attach this form or similar statement to his or her tax return **each year** the exemption is claimed.

You are the **custodial parent** if you had custody of the child for most of the year. You are the **noncustodial parent** if you had custody for a shorter period of time or did not have custody at all. For the definition of custody, see Pub. 501, Exemptions, Standard Deduction, and Filing Information.

Support test for children of divorced or separated parents. Generally, the custodial parent is treated as having provided over half of the child's support if:

• The child received over half of his or her total support for the year from one or both of the parents **and**

• The child was in the custody of one or both of the parents for more than half of the year.

Note: *Public assistance payments, such as Temporary Assistance for Needy Families (TANF), are not support provided by the parents.*

For this support test to apply, the parents must be one of the following:

• Divorced or legally separated under a decree of divorce or separate maintenance,

• Separated under a written separation agreement, **or**

• Living apart at all times during the last 6 months of the year.

Caution: *This support test does not apply to parents who never married each other.*

If the support test applies, and the other four dependency tests in your tax return

instruction booklet are also met, the custodial parent can claim the child's exemption.

Exception. The custodial parent will not be treated as having provided over half of the child's support if **any** of the following apply.

• The custodial parent agrees not to claim the child's exemption by signing this form or similar statement.

• The child is treated as having received over half of his or her total support from a person under a multiple support agreement (**Form 2120**, Multiple Support Declaration).

• A pre-1985 divorce decree or written separation agreement states that the noncustodial parent can claim the child as a dependent. But the noncustodial parent must provide at least $600 for the child's support during the year. This rule does not apply if the decree or agreement was changed after 1984 to say that the noncustodial parent cannot claim the child as a dependent.

Additional information. For more details, see Pub. 504, Divorced or Separated Individuals.

Specific Instructions

Custodial parent. You may agree to release your claim to the child's exemption for the current tax year or for future years, or both.

• Complete **Part I** if you agree to release your claim to the child's exemption for the current tax year.

• Complete **Part II** if you agree to release your claim to the child's exemption for any or all future years. If you do, write the specific future year(s) or "all future years" in the space provided in Part II.

 To help ensure future support, you may not want to release your claim to the child's exemption for future years.

Noncustodial parent. Attach this form or similar statement to your tax return for **each year** you claim the child's exemption. You may claim the exemption **only** if the other four dependency tests in your tax return instruction booklet are met.

Note: *If the custodial parent released his or her claim to the child's exemption for any future year, you **must** attach a copy of this form or similar statement to your tax return for each future year that you claim the exemption. Keep a copy for your records.*

Paperwork Reduction Act Notice. We ask for the information on this form to carry out the Internal Revenue laws of the United States. You are required to give us the information. We need it to ensure that you are complying with these laws and to allow us to figure and collect the right amount of tax.

You are not required to provide the information requested on a form that is subject to the Paperwork Reduction Act unless the form displays a valid OMB control number. Books or records relating to a form or its instructions must be retained as long as their contents may become material in the administration of any Internal Revenue law. Generally, tax returns and return information are confidential, as required by Internal Revenue Code section 6103.

The time needed to complete and file this form will vary depending on individual circumstances. The estimated average time is:

Recordkeeping	7 min.
Learning about the law or the form	5 min.
Preparing the form	7 min.
Copying, assembling, and sending the form to the IRS	14 min.

If you have comments concerning the accuracy of these time estimates or suggestions for making this form simpler, we would be happy to hear from you. You can write to the Tax Forms Committee, Western Area Distribution Center, Rancho Cordova, CA 95743-0001. **Do not** send the form to this address. Instead, see the Instructions for Form 1040 or Form 1040A.

Cat. No. 13910F		Form **8332** (Rev. 12-2000)

Appendix 10
Social Security Information Request

Form Approved
OMB No. 0960-0466

[ ] SP

Request for Earnings and Benefit Estimate Statement

[ ] Please check this box if you want to get your statement in Spanish instead of English.

Please print or type your answers. When you have completed the form, fold it and mail it to us. (If you prefer to send your request using the Internet, contact us at http://www.ssa.gov)

1. Name shown on your Social Security card:

_____ _____
First Name   Middle Initial

_____
Last Name Only

2. Your Social Security number as shown on your card:

[ ][ ][ ] - [ ][ ] - [ ][ ][ ][ ]

3. Your date of birth (Mo.-Day-Yr.)

[ ][ ] - [ ][ ] - [ ][ ]

4. Other Social Security numbers you have used:

[ ][ ][ ] - [ ][ ] - [ ][ ][ ][ ]

[ ][ ][ ] - [ ][ ] - [ ][ ][ ][ ]

5. Your sex: [ ] Male   [ ] Female

For items 6 and 8 show only earnings covered by Social Security. Do NOT include wages from State, local or Federal Government employment that are NOT covered for Social Security or that are covered ONLY by Medicare.

6. Show your actual earnings (wages and/or net self-employment income) for last year and your estimated earnings for this year.

A. Last year's actual earnings: (Dollars Only)

$ [ ][ ][ ] , [ ][ ][ ] . [0][0]

B. This year's estimated earnings: (Dollars Only)

$ [ ][ ][ ] , [ ][ ][ ] . [0][0]

7. Show the age at which you plan to stop working.

[ ][ ]
(Show only one age)

8. Below, show the average yearly amount (not your total future lifetime earnings) that you think you will earn between now and when you plan to stop working. Include performance or scheduled pay increases or bonuses, but not cost-of-living increases.

If you expect to earn significantly more or less in the future due to promotions, job changes, part-time work, or an absence from the work force, enter the amount that most closely reflects your future average yearly earnings.

If you don't expect any significant changes, show the same amount you are earning now (the amount in 6B).

Future average yearly earnings: (Dollars Only)

$ [ ][ ][ ] , [ ][ ][ ] . [0][0]

9. Do you want us to send the statement:
   • To you? Enter your name and mailing address.
   • To someone else (your accountant, pension plan, etc.)? Enter your name with "c/o" and the name and address of that person or organization.

_____
Name

_____
Street Address (Include Apt. No., P.O. Box, or Rural Route)

_____
City   State   Zip Code

Notice:
I am asking for information about my own Social Security record or the record of a person I am authorized to represent. I understand that if I deliberately request information under false pretenses, I may be guilty of a Federal crime and could be fined and/or imprisoned. I authorize you to use a contractor to send the statement of earnings and benefit estimates to the person named in item 9.

▲

Please sign your name (Do Not Print)

_____

_____
Date   (Area Code) Daytime Telephone No.

Form SSA-7004-SM Internet (6-98) Destroy prior editions

260

Request for Earnings and Benefit Estimate Statement

Thank you for requesting this statement.

After you complete and return this form, we will--within 4 to 6 weeks--send you:

- a record of your earnings history and an estimate of how much you have paid in Social Security taxes, and
- estimates of benefits you (and your family) may be eligible for now and in the future.

We're pleased to furnish you with this information and we hope you'll find it useful in planning your financial future.

Social Security is more than just a program for retired people. It helps people of all ages in many ways. Whether you're young or old, male or female, single or with a family--Social Security can help you when you need it most. It can help support your family in the event of your death and pay you benefits if you become severly disabled.

If you have questions about Social Security or this form, please call our toll-free number, 1-800-772-1213.

Kenneth S. Apfel

Kenneth S. Apfel
Commissioner of Social Security

Mailing Address

Social Security Administration
Wilkes Barre Data Operations Center
PO Box 7004
Wilkes Barre PA 18767-7004

About The Privacy Act

Social Security is allowed to collect the facts on this form under Section 205 of the Social Security Act. We need them to quickly identify your record and prepare the earnings statement you asked us for. Giving us these facts is voluntary. However, without them we may not be able to give you an earnings and benefit estimate statement. Neither the Social Security Administration nor its contractor will use the information for any other purpose.

Paperwork Reduction Act Notice and Time It Takes Statement

The Paperwork Reduction Act of 1995 requires us to notify you that this information collection is in accordance with the clearance requirements of section 3507 of the Paperwork Reduction Act of 1995. We may not conduct or sponsor, and you are not required to respond to, a collection of information unless it displays a valid OMB control number. We estimate that it will take you about 5 minutes to complete this form. This includes the time it will take to read the instructions, gather the necessary facts and fill out the form.

Appendix 11
Credit Report Request Letter

      The address of local and national credit bureau reporting firms is found in the Yellow Pages.

Name
Address
City, State, Zip

Date

        Credit Bureau
        Address
        City, State Zip

        Re: [First] [Middle Initial] [Maiden] [Last]
               SSN

        This is to request that a copy of my entire credit history/report be mailed to me at the above address. I have enclosed a check in the amount of $_____ to cover the cost of the report and shipping.

        Thank you in advance for your prompt response to my request.

                     Very truly yours,

        [Name]

Wood ◆ Shaw

Appendix 12
Estimated Monthly Living Expenses

EXPENSES	MONTHLY PAYMENT
FIXED EXPENSES	$
House payment	$
Insurance	$
Home	$
Automobile	$
Health	$
Life	$
Other	$
Taxes - Home	$
FLEXIBLE EXPENSES	$
Electricity	$
Gas or Oil (Heat)	$
Telephone	$
Water and Sewer	$
Cable Television	$
Pest Control	$
Yard Care	$
Household Help	$
Repair/Maintenance	$
Other	$
FOOD	$
Groceries	$
Restaurants	$
Lunches	$
TRANSPORTATION	$
Car payment	$
Gas and Oil	$
Repairs/Maintenance	$
Auto Tag and Taxes	$
CHILDREN	$
Private School, Tutors, etc.	$
Activities (Sports, Music, Scouts, etc)	$
School lunches	$
Other school costs	$
CLOTHING/PERSONAL	$
Clothes - You	$
Clothes - Children	$
Shoes	$
Accessories	$
Laundry/Dry Cleaning	$
Beauty Shop/Barber	$
Cosmetics	$
ENTERTAINMENT	$
Newspapers	$
Magazines, Books	$
Sports, Movies, etc.	$
Vacations	$
Other Entertainment	$
EDUCATION	$
Tuition	$
Textbooks, Notebooks, Binders, etc.	$
MISCELLANEOUS COSTS/EXPENSES	$
Religious Contribution	$

Gifts (Birthdays, Holidays, etc.)	$
Taxes Withheld	$
Savings	$
IRA, Other Retirement	$
MEDICAL	$
Doctors	$
Dentists	$
Orthodontist	$
Optometrist	$
Medicine/Prescriptions	$
Other	$
CREDIT CARDS (Itemize with Balance Due)	Minimum Payment
	$
	$
	$
	$
	$
PERSONAL LOANS (Itemize)	$
	$
OTHER	$
	$
TOTAL EXPENSES	$
TOTAL PERSONAL NET INCOME	$
ALIMONY PAYMENTS	$
CHILD SUPPORT PAYMENTS	$
SURPLUS OR DEFICIT	$

Appendix 13
Estimated Child Support Expenses

FIXED EXPENSES			MONTHLY PAYMENT
House payment or rent			
Insurance:			
Homeowner's Insurance			
Automobile			
Health			
Life			
Other			
Taxes - Home			
FLEXIBLE EXPENSES			
Electricity			
Gas or Oil (Heat)			
Telephone			
Water and Sewer			
Lawn Maintenance			
Cable Television			
Pest Control			
Household Help			
Repair/Maintenance			
Other			
FOOD			
Groceries			
Restaurants			
Lunches			
TRANSPORTATION			
Car Payment			
Gas & oil			
Repairs/Maintenance			
Tag/Taxes			
CHILDREN			
Medical			
Dental/Orthodontist			
Prescription Medications			
Clothes			
Shoes			
Accessories			
Haircuts			
Tuition			
Lunches			
Extra-Curricular (Sports, Music, Dance, Tutors)			
Gifts (Birthday parties; Holiday parties)			
Day Care/After-School Care			
Camp			
PERSONAL			
Clothing			
Shoes			
Accessories			
Laundry/Dry Cleaning			
Haircuts			
Cosmetics			
MEDICAL			
Doctors			
Dentists			
Optometrist			

Medicine/Prescriptions			
ENTERTAINMENT			
Newspapers/Magazines/Books			
Movies/Video Rentals			
Vacations			
Theater			
MISCELLANEOUS			
Religious Contribution			
Charitable Contributions			
Gifts (Birthdays, Holidays, etc.)			
Savings			
IRA, other Retirement			
Postage			
Memberships			
Other			
TOTAL EXPENSES			

Wood ◆ Shaw

Appendix 14
Post-Divorce Checklist

Checklist	Needs to be Done	Completed
Appeal Deadline: 42 days from entry of Final Judgment of Divorce		
Prepare Deeds and File		
Real Property Deeds		
Estate Documents		
Will		
Medical Directive		
Power of Attorney		
Name Change (Probate Court)		
Automobile Titles		
Automobile Insurance		
Insurance Forms		
Life Insurance Provisions - Notify Carrier of Beneficiary Change		
Health Insurance Provisions - Notify carrier and order new identification card(s)		
Bank Accounts		
Safety Deposit Box		
Tax-IRS Forms		
IRS Form 8332 (Dependency Exemption)		
Form W-4		
Retirement Accounts / IRA / Pension		
QDRO		
Income Withholding Orders		

Saving Your Assets

Appendix 15
Child Support Forms

State of Alabama Unified Judicial System	**CHILD SUPPORT OBLIGATION INCOME STATEMENT/AFFIDAVIT**	Case Number
Form CS-41 Rev. 10/93		

IN THE _____ COURT OF _____ COUNTY

Plaintiff_____ v.   Defendant

AFFIDAVIT

I, _____, being duly sworn upon my oath, state as follows:

1. I am the ____ plaintiff ____ defendant in the above-entitled matter.
    My Social Security Number is:

2. I am _____ currently employed. My employer's name and address is:

    _____ not currently employed.
    My last employer's name and address is:

    Last position title:
    Average monthly salary last year of employment:

3. My gross monthly income includes:
    Employment income   _____
    Self-employment income   _____
    Other employment-related income   _____
    Other non-employment-related income   _____
    Total   _____

    3.a. I incur the following amount monthly for child care   _____
    3.b. The child(ren) of the parties is/are

    _____ not covered by health insurance from me
    and/or my employer

    _____ covered by health insurance and I pay the
    Following amount for the insurance coverage

4. I understand that I will be required to maintain all income documentation used in preparing this affidavit (including my most recent income tax return) and that such documentation shall be made available as directed by the Court.

5. I understand that any intentional falsification of the information presented in this income statement/affidavit shall be deemed contempt of court.

                                                            Affiant
Sworn to and subscribed before me this
day of _____, _____.

Notary/Clerk/Register

Wood ◆ Shaw

State of Alabama Unified Judicial System Form CS-42 Rev. 10/93	CHILD SUPPORT OBLIGATION INCOME STATEMENT/AFFIDAVIT	Case Number

| IN THE _____ | COURT OF _____ COUNTY |

_____ v. _____
Plaintiff   **Defendant**

Children	Date of Birth	Children	Date of Birth

	Plaintiff	Defendant	Combined
1. **MONTHLY GROSS INCOME**	$	$	
a. Minus Preexisting Child Support Payment	-	-	
b. Minus Preexisting Periodic Alimony Payment	-	-	
2. **MONTHLY ADJUSTED GROSS INCOME**	$	$	$
3. **PERCENTAGE SHARE OF INCOME** (Each parent's income on Line 2 divided by the Combined Income	%	%	
4. **BASIC CHILD SUPPORT OBLIGATION** [Apply Line 2 Combined to "schedule of basic child support obligations" (Appendix to Rule 32)]			$
5. **WORK-RELATED CHILD CARE COSTS**			$
6. **HEALTH INSURANCE COSTS**			$
7. **TOTAL CHILD SUPPORT OBLIGATION** (Add lines 4, 5, and 6)			$
8. **EACH PARENT'S CHILD SUPPORT OBLIGATION** (Multiply Line 7 by Line 3)	$	$	
9. **ADJUSTMENT FOR PAYMENT OF HEALTH INSURANCE** (If obligor pays health insurance, enter amount paid in obligor's column)	$	$	
10. **RECOMMENDED CHILD SUPPORT ORDER** (Subtract Line 9 from the amount on Line 8. Leave custodial parent's column blank.)	$	$	

Comment, Calculations, or Rebuttals to Guidelines:

PREPARED BY:	DATE:

269

State of Alabama Unified Judicial System	**CHILD SUPPORT OBLIGATION INCOME STATEMENT/AFFIDAVIT**	Case Number
Form CS-43 Rev. 10/93		

IN THE _____ **COURT OF**
COUNTY

_____v.
          Plaintiff   **Defendant**

- Based upon the income and expenditures supplied by parties in Form CS-41, "Child Support Obligation Income Statement/Affidavit," the child support guidelines, as set out in Rule 32, Alabama Rules of Judicial Administration, have been followed and applied.

- The child support guidelines, as set out in Rule 32, Alabama Rules of Judicial Administration, have not been followed and applied because of the following reasons:

Date:_____   Date:_____

_____
Signature of Plaintiff

_____   Signature of Defendant

                  AOC#:_____AOC#:
Signature of Plaintiff's Attorney   Signature of Defendant's Attorney

_____
Address of Plaintiff or Plaintiff's Attorney   Address of Defendant or Defendant's Attorney

_____
Telephone No. of Plaintiff or Plaintiff's Attorney   Telephone No. of Defendant or Defendant's Attorney

W o o d ◆ S h a w

State of Alabama Unified Judicial System Sample Form Rev. 9/97	**INFORMATION SHEET** **(Child Support Reform Act of 1997)**	**CASE NUMBER**

IN THE CIRCUIT COURT OF JEFFERSON COUNTY, ALABAMA

_____v.

Plaintiff   Defendant

------- Not Applicable, No child(dren) a party to or subject to this action

Information Concerning the Parties:	Information Concerning the Parties:
Plaintiff (Mother, Father, Other_____, or Other Party (Specify) (_ _____)	Plaintiff (Mother, Father, Other_____, or Other Party (Specify) (_ _____)
Address (including City, State and Zip Code):	Address (including City, State and Zip Code):
Telephone Number: Home (____)	Telephone Number: Home (____)
SSN:	SSN:
Race: _____ Sex:	Race: _____ Sex:
Place of Employment and Address (including City, State and Zip Code (if applicable)	Place of Employment and Address (including City, State and Zip Code (if applicable)
Work Telephone Number (____)	Work Telephone Number (____)

INFORMATION CONCERNING THE CHILDREN

Name	Address(es)	Sex	DOB (dd/mm/yy)	SSN

THE CHILD SUPPORT REFORM ACT OF 1997 REQUIRES THAT THE COURT MAINTAIN THE ABOVE INFORMATION IN THE RECORD FOR ALL PARTIES WHO MAY EITHER INITIATE AN ACTION OR INTERVENE IN AN EXISTING ACTION.

Completed by: WOOD & SHAW, L.L.C._____Date Completed:
                Print name   Daytime Phone (205) 871-9550

271

Saving Your Assets

Appendix 16
Schedule of Basic Child Support Obligations

NUMBER OF CHILDREN DUE SUPPORT

COMBINED GROSS INCOME	ONE CHILD	TWO CHILDREN	THREE CHILDREN	FOUR CHILDREN	FIVE CHILDREN	SIX CHILDREN
Below 550.00 Monthly Basic Child Support Obligation Established at the Discretion of the Court						
550.00	50	51	51	52	52	53
600.00	82	83	84	85	86	87
650.00	112	113	114	115	116	118
700.00	141	142	144	145	147	148
750.00	151	172	173	175	177	179
800.00	158	201	203	205	208	210
850.00	166	230	233	235	238	240
900.00	173	259	262	265	268	271
950.00	180	279	291	294	298	301
1000.00	187	290	320	324	327	331
1050.00	194	301	350	354	357	361
1100.00	201	312	379	383	387	391
1150.00	208	323	405	413	417	422
1200.00	215	334	418	442	447	452
1250.00	222	345	432	472	477	482
1300.00	229	356	445	502	508	514
1350.00	236	367	459	518	543	549
1400.00	243	378	474	534	577	584
1450.00	251	390	488	550	599	618
1500.00	257	399	500	564	614	648
1550.00	263	409	512	577	629	672

1600.00	269	418	524	590	643	688
1650.00	275	428	536	604	658	704
1700.00	281	437	548	617	672	719
1750.00	287	447	560	631	687	735
1800.00	294	456	571	644	701	750
1850.00	300	466	583	657	716	766
1900.00	306	475	595	671	730	781
1950.00	312	485	607	684	745	797
2000.00	318	495	619	698	760	813
2050.00	325	505	632	712	775	829
2100.00	331	514	644	726	790	846
2150.00	338	524	656	740	806	862
2200.00	344	534	669	754	821	878
2250.00	350	544	681	768	836	894
2300.00	357	554	694	782	852	911
2350.00	363	563	705	795	865	925
2400.00	368	572	716	807	879	940
2450.00	374	580	727	819	893	954
2500.00	380	589	738	832	906	969
2550.00	386	598	749	844	920	983
2600.00	391	607	760	857	933	998
2650.00	397	616	771	869	947	1012
2700.00	403	625	782	882	961	1027
2750.00	409	633	793	894	974	1042
2800.00	414	642	804	907	988	1056
2850.00	420	651	815	919	1002	1071
2900.00	426	660	826	931	1015	1085
2950.00	431	669	837	944	1029	1100
3000.00	437	677	848	956	1042	1114
3050.00	443	686	859	969	1056	1129

3100.00	449	695	870	981	1070	1143
3150.00	454	704	881	994	1083	1158
3200.00	459	712	891	1005	1096	1171
3250.00	464	720	901	1016	1108	1185
3300.00	469	728	911	1028	1121	1198
3350.00	475	736	922	1039	1133	1211
3400.00	480	745	932	1050	1145	1225
3450.00	485	753	942	1062	1158	1238
3500.00	490	761	952	1073	1170	1252
3550.00	495	769	962	1085	1183	1265
3600.00	500	777	972	1096	1195	1278
3650.00	505	785	982	1107	1208	1292
3700.00	511	794	994	1120	1222	1307
3750.00	517	803	1005	1133	1236	1322
3800.00	523	813	1017	1146	1250	1337
3850.00	529	822	1028	1159	1264	1352
3900.00	534	831	1040	1172	1278	1367
3950.00	540	840	1051	1185	1293	1382
4000.00	546	849	1063	1197	1307	1397
4050.00	552	858	1074	1210	1321	1412
4100.00	558	868	1085	1223	1335	1427
4150.00	563	877	1097	1236	1349	1443
4200.00	569	886	1108	1249	1363	1458
4250.00	575	895	1120	1262	1377	1473
4300.00	581	904	1131	1275	1391	1488
4350.00	587	913	1143	1288	1405	1503
4400.00	592	923	1154	1300	1419	1518
4450.00	598	931	1159	1313	1433	1532
4500.00	604	940	1170	1325	1446	1546
4550.00	609	948	1180	1337	1458	1560
4600.00	614	956	1190	1348	1471	1573

4650.00	619	964	1200	1359	1483	1586
4700.00	624	972	1209	1370	1495	1598
4750.00	629	980	1219	1381	1507	1611
4800.00	635	987	1229	1392	1519	1624
4850.00	640	995	1239	1403	1531	1637
4900.00	645	1003	1249	1414	1543	1650
4950.00	650	1011	1258	1425	1555	1663
5000.00	655	1019	1268	1436	1567	1676
5050.00	660	1027	1278	1447	1579	1689
5100.00	665	1035	1288	1458	1591	1701
5150.00	670	1042	1298	1469	1604	1714
5200.00	675	1050	1307	1481	1616	1727
5250.00	681	1058	1317	1492	1628	1740
5300.00	686	1066	1327	1503	1640	1753
5350.00	691	1074	1337	1514	1652	1766
5400.00	696	1082	1346	1525	1664	1779
5450.00	701	1090	1356	1536	1676	1792
5500.00	706	1097	1366	1547	1688	1805
5550.00	711	1105	1376	1558	1700	1817
5600.00	716	1113	1386	1569	1712	1830
5650.00	722	1121	1395	1580	1724	1843
5700.00	727	1129	1405	1591	1737	1856
5750.00	732	1137	1415	1602	1749	1869
5800.00	737	1145	1425	1613	1761	1882
5850.00	742	1152	1435	1624	1773	1895
5900.00	747	1160	1444	1636	1785	1908
5950.00	752	1168	1454	1647	1797	1920
6000.00	757	1176	1464	1658	1809	1933
6050.00	762	1184	1474	1669	1821	1946
6100.00	768	1192	1483	1680	1833	1959
6150.00	772	1198	1497	1689	1843	1969
6200.00	775	1203	1504	1697	1851	1979

Saving Your Assets

6250.00	779	1209	1511	1705	1860	1988
6300.00	783	1214	1518	1713	1869	1997
6350.00	787	1220	1526	1721	1878	2007
6400.00	790	1226	1533	1729	1886	2016
6450.00	794	1231	1540	1737	1895	2025
6500.00	798	1237	1547	1745	1904	2035
6550.00	802	1243	1554	1753	1913	2044
6600.00	805	1248	1561	1761	1922	2053
6650.00	809	1254	1568	1769	1930	2063
6700.00	813	1259	1575	1777	1939	2072
6750.00	817	1265	1582	1785	1948	2081
6800.00	820	1271	1589	1793	1957	2091
6850.00	824	1276	1597	1801	1965	2100
6900.00	828	1282	1604	1809	1974	2110
6950.00	831	1287	1611	1817	1983	2119
7000.00	835	1293	1618	1825	1992	2128
7050.00	839	1299	1625	1833	2000	2138
7100.00	843	1304	1632	1841	2009	2147
7150.00	846	1310	1639	1849	2018	2156
7200.00	850	1315	1646	1857	2027	2166
7250.00	854	1321	1653	1865	2035	2175
7300.00	857	1326	1660	1872	2043	2183
7350.00	860	1331	1666	1878	2050	2191
7400.00	862	1336	1672	1885	2057	2199
7450.00	865	1340	1678	1891	2064	2207
7500.00	868	1345	1684	1898	2072	2214
7550.00	871	1350	1690	1904	2079	2222
7600.00	874	1355	1696	1911	2086	2230
7650.00	877	1359	1702	1917	2093	2238
7700.00	879	1364	1708	1924	2100	2246
7750.00	882	1369	1714	1930	2107	2254

Wood ◆ Shaw

7800.00	885	1374	1720	1937	2114	2261
7850.00	888	1378	1726	1943	2122	2269
7900.00	891	1383	1732	1950	2129	2277
7950.00	894	1388	1738	1956	2136	2285
8000.00	896	1393	1744	1962	2143	2293
8050.00	899	1397	1750	1969	2150	2300
8100.00	902	1402	1756	1975	2157	2308
8150.00	905	1407	1762	1982	2164	2316
8200.00	908	1412	1768	1988	2171	2324
8250.00	911	1417	1774	1995	2179	2332
8300.00	914	1421	1780	2001	2186	2340
8350.00	916	1426	1785	2008	2193	2347
8400.00	919	1431	1792	2014	2200	2355
8450.00	922	1434	1797	2020	2206	2361
8500.00	924	1438	1801	2025	2212	2367
8550.00	926	1441	1806	2030	2217	2373
8600.00	929	1445	1810	2035	2222	2379
8650.00	931	1448	1815	2040	2228	2384
8700.00	933	1452	1819	2045	2233	2390
8750.00	935	1455	1823	2050	2239	2396
8800.00	938	1459	1828	2055	2244	2401
8850.00	940	1462	1832	2060	2249	2407
8900.00	942	1466	1837	2065	2255	2413
8950.00	945	1469	1841	2070	2260	2418
9000.00	947	1473	1846	2075	2266	2424
9050.00	949	1476	1850	2080	2271	2430
9100.00	951	1480	1854	2085	2276	2435
9150.00	954	1483	1859	2090	2282	2441
9200.00	956	1487	1863	2095	2287	2447
9250.00	958	1490	1868	2100	2293	2453
9300.00	961	1494	1872	2105	2298	2458

Saving Your Assets

9350.00	963	1497	1876	2110	2303	2464
9400.00	965	1501	1881	2115	2309	2470
9450.00	967	1504	1885	2120	2314	2475
9500.00	970	1507	1890	2125	2320	2481
9550.00	972	1511	1894	2130	2325	2487
9600.00	974	1514	1898	2135	2330	2492
9650.00	977	1518	1903	2140	2336	2498
9700.00	979	1521	1907	2145	2341	2504
9750.00	981	1525	1912	2150	2347	2510
9800.00	983	1528	1916	2155	2352	2515
9850.00	986	1532	1921	2160	2357	2521
9900.00	988	1535	1925	2165	2363	2527
9950.00	990	1539	1929	2170	2368	2532
10000.00	992	1542	1934	2175	2374	2538

Wood ◆ Shaw

Paul B. Shaw, Jr., (left) and John M. Wood are partners in
the Birmingham, Alabama law firm of Wood & Shaw,
L.L.C. Their practice is devoted almost exclusively
to matrimonial law.

The two attorney/authors are available to speak to groups
all across Alabama on the financial aspects of family law.

They can be reached at Wood & Shaw, L.L.C., 2924
Crescent Avenue, Birmingham, Alabama 35209.
Telephone 205/871-9550, Fax 205/871-9549,
email: john@woodandshaw.com
paul@woodandshaw.com
website: www.woodandshaw.com